Developing a Winning Grant Proposal

In a world of tightening budgets and increased competition for grant money, *Developing a Winning Grant Proposal* provides the guidelines, strategies, plans and techniques to craft a fundable grant proposal. A user-friendly, engaging and up-to-date guide, this book covers the entire process from the inception of a good idea, to the formulation of a strong proposal, to the next steps once a proposal is funded. Providing a basic overview and helpful tools for busy faculty and researchers, this is a must-have guide for anyone interested in the mechanisms that successful grant-writers employ.

Special features include:

- Appendices with a "Model of a Funded Proposal" and a "Basic 'Toolbox' for Grant-Seekers"
- Checklists for self-evaluating the efficacy of each portion of the grant proposal
- Coverage of complex issues in a concise and clear manner, perfect for grant-writers facing tight time constraints.

Donald C. Orlich is Professor Emeritus of Education and Science Instruction at Washington State University, USA.

Nancy R. Shrope is Assistant Director of the Office of Grant and Research Development at Washington State University, USA.

Developing a Winning Grant Proposal

Donald C. Orlich and
Nancy R. Shrope

Routledge
Taylor & Francis Group

NEW YORK AND LONDON

First published 2013
by Routledge
711 Third Avenue, New York, NY 10017

Simultaneously published in the UK
by Routledge
2 Park Square, Milton Park, Abingdon, Oxon OX14 4RN

Routledge is an imprint of the Taylor & Francis Group, an informa business

© 2013 Taylor & Francis

The right of Donald C. Orlich and Nancy R. Shrope to be identified as authors of this work has been asserted by them in accordance with sections 77 and 78 of the Copyright, Designs and Patents Act 1988.

Library of Congress Cataloging in Publication Data
Orlich, Donald C.
    Developing a winning grant proposal/Donald C. Orlich,
    Nancy R. Shrope.
    p. cm.
    Includes bibliographical references and index.
    1. Proposal writing for grants.   2. Fund raising.
    I. Shrope, Nancy R.   II. Title.
    HG177.O75 2012
    658.15'224—dc23
    2012012566

ISBN: 978-0-415-53534-2 (hbk)
ISBN: 978-0-415-53535-9 (pbk)
ISBN: 978-0-203-11263-2 (ebk)

Typeset in Perpetua and Bell Gothic
by Florence Production Ltd, Stoodleigh, Devon

SUSTAINABLE FORESTRY INITIATIVE
Certified Sourcing
www.sfiprogram.org
SFI-00555
The SFI label applies to the text stock.

Printed and bound in the United States of America by Walsworth Publishing Company, Marceline, MO.

Contents

Preface

Developing a Winning Grant Proposal was designed to help grant proposal writers understand the realities associated with this often time-consuming and monumental task. This concise book is for individuals who are seeking outside grant support. The resources include local, state and federal governmental sources, federal agencies, businesses, charitable groups and foundations. We provide current references with the latest tools of the information age to help identify grant sources. There are tested models, strategies, techniques, methods and checklists provided by which to obtain those difficult grant funds.

This work has had extensive field-testing and reviews. Your authors have conducted numerous proposal-writing workshops locally, regionally and internationally using this book's format. By using this book, proposal writers will find many tips that will help in designing a clearly written and successful proposal.

Intended Audiences. *Developing a Winning Grant Proposal* is designed to help time-strapped professors, teachers, researchers, administrators and non-profit foundational personnel with time-saving tips and models. Further, it is organized for use in courses that focus on grant proposal preparation. We show how an idea can be systematically organized and transferred into an appropriate proposal, which is relevant to all these audiences.

Basic Features. Our hallmark is to treat each topic in just enough depth by providing operational examples without overwhelming the reader, as do many of the current tomes in this genre. Each chapter is structured to illustrate and follow the basic sections of most grant guidelines and proposals. For example, Chapter 1 is about developing proposals. Chapter 2 then explores how to monitor funding sources. Chapter 3 discusses needs assessments. Chapter 4 models the initial elements of a proposal. Chapter 5 shows how to construct the work plan of a proposal. Chapter 6 is all about budgeting principles. Chapter 7 focuses specifically on grant proposals for conducting research. Chapter 8 relates to classroom types of proposals. Chapter 9 takes you through the submission processes. Chapter 10 details how one implements a funded project. Appendix A is a replica of a funded project and Appendix B is a "toolbox" providing details of where one can search for selected and current sources of funding.

Each chapter opens with an outline of the topics treated. The chapters contain models and detailed checklists to aid in the task of preparing the most fundable proposal.

We illustrate how one searches for exactly the "right" agency or foundation to which the proposal should be submitted. The critical importance of following the particular funding agency's guidelines is stressed throughout. The roadblocks that grant proposal writers face are amply illustrated with time-tested suggestions and illustrations on how to avoid them. We urge all grant-seekers to prepare their own writing timeline to meet those dreaded deadlines. Additionally, the book addresses how proposals may be revised and resubmitted. We also urge any grant proposal writer to have colleagues review their penultimate draft to identify any problems before submission. In all aspects of the book we attempt to engage you, the reader.

We also thank our colleagues, Esther Pratt and Diane Rathbun, in the Office of Grant and Research Development, Washington State University, for their help and support, and Sandra Tyke for preparing the original manuscript.

We wish you $uccess in your efforts.

And, now on to Chapter 1—"Developing a Proposal."

Developing a Proposal

CHAPTER SUMMARY

- Some Basic Elements
- Communicating Your Intentions
- Priorities
- Writing Big Proposals
- Checklist for Big Proposal Development

You can be a successful grant proposal writer if you follow three rather simple steps. First, you need a good idea. Second, you locate a source that has already funded similar ideas. Third, you design, craft and develop your idea into a *well-written* statement. Notice the emphasis is on *well written*. Successful grant-writers are those persons who carefully prepare their proposals. It is a very time-consuming task, but that effort will reap rewards. And now that we have the basic rudiments established, how do you go about this process in a systematic and business-like manner?

One assumption that underlies this book is that you will write proposals for some time into the future. That is, you will become one of the thousands who write grant proposals as a regular part of your job. The process becomes one of a journey rather than a singular event. Since getting there is half the fun, you need to develop a systematic process of knowing what is being funded, who is willing to fund your proposals and how to find this information.

SOME BASIC ELEMENTS

Virtually all grant-funding agencies, foundations or businesses require the same generic elements in the grant proposal. The exact details may vary, but the basic elements tend to be similar whether it is a multimillion-dollar proposal to the National Science Foundation or a $500 proposal to the local utility company. Below is a list of the basic elements in a proposal.

Basic Elements of a Proposal

- Cover Sheet
- Table of Contents
- Project Summary or Abstract
- Introduction
- Problem Statement or Needs Assessment
- Project Description or Program Design
  - Goal
  - Objectives and Significance
  - Methodology
  - Evaluation and Assessment
  - Timeline
- Results from Prior Support
- Broader Impact Statement
- Facilities, Equipment and Resources
- Personnel
- Bibliography
- Biographical Sketches
- Budget
- Budget Justification
- Current and Pending Support
- Supporting Materials

Let us briefly explore these critical elements and then spend the remaining chapters expanding each section and their subcategories.

The Introduction

Begin your proposal with a statement that captures the full attention of the reviewer. An introduction sets the stage for the remainder of the proposal. Remember, you are communicating your ideas through a one-way medium: *writing*. The best proposals—make that the *best-written* proposals—get funded in every competition. Therefore, you need to spend a great deal of time and effort in carefully selecting the exact wording. Every word or sentence must carry an explicit connotation and explicit denotation. Vagueness in writing yields only letters of declinations. You will spend a good deal of time developing a proposal, and in most cases you will rewrite sections so explicitly that there can be no mistake in your intent.

A Need or Problem

The second basic element for all proposals is to identify the need being addressed or the problem being solved. If you address a need, you will have to provide data to support it. Chapter 3 provides a systematic approach to identifying needs and how to conduct a needs assessment.

The need statement of a proposal is best concluded with a statement of significance. Just how significant is this proposal to the group on which you are focusing the proposed efforts? Don't be modest. Keep in mind you will tend to write a proposal to an unknown evaluation panel. Most likely, none of the panel members will know you or your institution. So, you must provide instant rapport in the first two sections of the proposal.

Goals and Objectives

The third basic element contains your goals statement. The current vogue of many funding groups is the requirement to incorporate a vision statement. The goal or vision tends to be broad, global statements. However, they do differ, as you will see later in Chapter 4. A listing of the exact objectives that you intend to accomplish as a consequence of being funded then follows the goals.

Procedures

The fourth major element is the body of the proposal or the narrative section. This element may be called procedures, methodology, activities or the work plan. However the particular guidelines ask you to name them, you label them thusly. This element is about providing details, details and more details. In this section, you elaborate how each objective will be attained. You answer the five Ws—who, what, when, where and why.

Typically, in the procedures section, you will also list how the project is organized and who are the instructional or research team members.

Evaluation

The fifth basic element of a proposal is usually the evaluation model that you will employ. As the proposal writer, you select the most appropriate model of evaluation that coincides with your objectives once your proposal has been funded and the study has been completed. The basic idea of evaluating a project is to determine how well and to what extent you successfully met the project's objectives. Chapter 5 discusses evaluation and management plans in detail.

Budget

The sixth element of our generic model is the budget. This section provides a general expenditure (investment) plan and is followed by specific details on how the general costs were determined. The latter are known as "budget justifications" and are not equivalent to the budget figures or numbers.

Basically, that is all that there is to it. In nearly all cases, the funder provides a general set of guidelines that specifies the order in which these basic elements will be written. *Always follow the guidelines!* No matter how redundant or even silly you may think a set of guidelines may be, you must follow them. Reviewers of your proposal will. If you deviate from the guidelines, then you'll be penalized and, more than likely, not funded. It is *their* money, so follow their directions with the utmost care.

COMMUNICATING YOUR INTENTIONS

By now you are probably thinking, "The authors are really over-stressing the theme of carefully writing a proposal." When writing, crafting, developing, preparing a grant proposal, you must communicate your intentions in such a manner that they cannot be misinterpreted by any of the proposal reviewers. For the most part, review panels are composed of people just like you. They are typically selected to provide a wide spectrum of experiences and backgrounds. You should write so carefully that they do not have to interpret your intentions. The more explicit your writing, the easier it is for the review panel members to understand your intentions.

How do you state a problem? That element needs to be expanded.

Using the Problem as a Guide

The careful crafting of the problem statement is most essential, for it will be one of the first sections to be read by a reviewer. If the problem is to eliminate illiteracy in North America, then you'll need billions of dollars. If the problem relates to inadequate reading skills for children in a specific elementary school, then $20,000 might be adequate to fund a pilot project. The key point is not the statement of the problem, per se, but stating a problem that is manageable and solvable.

A problem is a condition that requires some extra effort to fix. A problem can be a brief statement of an observation. For example, a common problem that is frequently observed is that preadolescent girls do not achieve as well as expected in science. The problem is not that all girls do not achieve as expected. It is a condition focused on a specific group, under a specific context. So, we might write a statement such as the following:

Teachers in our middle school are often unaware that they may be biased against young female students in science classes. As a consequence, girls report being more negatively inclined toward science than are young males. In actual classroom observations, we have found that teachers reward boys more than girls in science classes and that girl-initiated science interactions decline during middle school years. Finally, teacher expectations tend to favor boys. From these observations come two distinct, but related, problems: (1) How can science teachers be made aware of the bias toward girls; and (2) What types of training intervention can eliminate sexual bias in middle school science classes?

Reread the above statement. Observe how the problem begins with a rather broadly stated issue and then culminates with a very specific, but solvable problem statement. This is called "V" writing. By giving some general background, the reader or reviewer in the case of grant proposals, is given enough information to make a smooth transition into a specific condition. You will also observe that the statement is specific and explicit.

In contrast, read the following statement in Exhibit "P" that described a problem.

EXHIBIT "P": The Problem

Home weatherization is not the sole determinant of household energy usage. People's habits can, and do, have serious implications for environmental sustainability. To be effective, conservation education programs must be holistic. Typically, such programs focus on adult consumers with little or no consideration given to the youth who are the future consumer.

Cheap electricity has been one of the key factors that has defined the economic opportunities, environment and quality of life in the state of . . . As a result of the increased consumption of electricity, the decade-long surplus of electric energy has disappeared.

To meet this challenge, the state has developed a broad base energy strategy. An important goal of this strategy is to educate not only the adult consumer, but children as well. As the future consumers of energy, they need to be aware of its monetary and environmental costs. Today it is known that stretching electricity supplies by improving efficiency not only reduces the need for new power plants, but it is also less expensive, less polluting, and avoids the environmental impact of new power plants.

Energy conservation education is a component of the . . . Project. The Project includes educational and support groups which enhance the knowledge of home energy conservation, resource allocation and other pertinent management issues for low-income families.

Developing an energy literate consumer who will make the right choices regarding their energy needs can only be brought about through conservation education. This, in turn, will contribute to the achievement of the conservation goals. By combining energy education with low-income weatherization and budget management . . . helps their clients to decrease their energy usage and increase both their ability to pay and their personal comfort.

How many times did you have to reread either part or all of that statement? The statement is confusing. You are not exactly certain what the problem might be or what parts of the problem will be addressed. Needless to say, the proposal that contained this description was not funded.

A problem needs to be written so that it is clear and concise. As was illustrated previously, the section containing the problem should be carefully prepared to lead a reviewer from a point of knowing little or nothing about a specific condition to a rather informed state. Listed below are a few problem statements that illustrate a straightforward approach.

- Children who attend schools in lower socio-economic neighborhoods have very limited access to personal computers in their classrooms.
- Volunteers for mathematics tutoring need additional training in the use of math manipulatives.
- The "Reading Recovery Program" is addressing only 40 percent of those needing the service.
- The history program lacks the instructional resources required to meet the "Expectations of Excellence" of the National Council for the Social Studies.
- Teacher education programs find it increasingly difficult to provide student teachers and interns with ethnic and multicultural experiences.
- Science teaching in grades K-6 focuses on factual or didactic instruction rather than on an inquiry model.

The above are illustrations of either training or developmental projects. When preparing proposals that are research oriented, you can use other styles. The first below is stated as a problem. The second example is a series of questions. Those are followed by two other examples.

- The major problems associated with clinical blood separation processes for obtaining white blood cells and platelets are low yields, lack of uniformity and purity of yields, and the length of procedures.
- What is the sequence of sensory-motor development leading to complex manipulative abilities? What is the timing of development of manipulative behaviors? What is the role of social context with development of these behaviors?

- During the past six academic years, the school district has experienced a 234 percent increase in reported child abuse cases. The number of cases has increased from 237 to 554. These abused children need extended care to be fully rehabilitated.
- There is not, however, a comprehensive and realistic model describing the dynamic interactions, which transfer energy and momentum of wind waves to motions of other frequencies or wave numbers.

Statements of the problem serve as the primary focus of the proposal. All the other proposal elements provide support showing how you will address it. Of course, you may state more than one problem. But a word of caution is needed here. If you begin to list several problems to be addressed, then there is a tendency by the panel members to conclude that too much is being attempted and they will rank the proposal lower. Perhaps the best advice is to focus on one major problem. Then the panel members know that the proposal is addressing one solvable issue.

Vision Statement

There are a few foundations and agencies that require a "vision" statement. Regardless of how you personally feel about the usefulness of vision statements, if a guideline even hints at one, prepare it. But a vision statement is not a singular production. You will have to meet with others in your organization to either prepare one or use the official statement that usually appears in your organization's handbook or guidelines.

For example, your institution or school district may be forecasting the future to be one that will be high-tech in nature. Perhaps major capital outlays are being made for computers, laser disk players, multimedia and peripheral equipment. You'll need to show a funder that there is a vision statement framing these intentions. It might read as follows.

Vision. Our public schools progress through the 21st Century with a vision of what education is becoming. A paradigm shift is taking place in learning and teaching that requires the schools to create a supportive environment that combines the best of our cultures and incorporates the unpredictability of the future. Affecting the "new" is the entire realm of technology that now permeates the disciplines of science, mathematics and engineering. The new educational paradigm creates the expectations that the future requires all students to attain skills that are technologically driven. That drive encompasses the entire spectrum of school learning and also adds to it a dimension that provides life skills which are needed in the home, the work place and the community at large.

Mathematics, science and technology teachers are key players in applying the basic tenets of the paradigm shift. As educators, we must view the disciplines as being highly interconnected. Several themes and problems require broad based knowledge to either understand or solve. This does not negate the necessity for specific knowledge bases, but acknowledges how understanding and application of these knowledge bases leads to even greater understanding and a better appreciation for real problem solving.

The above is certainly a noble forecasting of the future and would aid in driving future programs. Other visions may not be so elaborate. A few shorter examples suffice.

- The vision we have for our classes is an environment that stimulates the best achievement that each individual can make and yet stresses the small-group cooperation so widely needed in our post-industrial workforce.
- Our vision is to prepare administrators who understand the positive interactions of a diverse society and who can enhance the human potential of all who are impacted by our organization.
- The vision guiding this project is that all children can learn. We honor learning and the basic educational and human values associated with the attainment of higher-order thinking skills.
- Through successful fruition of this project, we have the opportunity to create a safe and orderly environment in our high school.

The vision statement is a perception that guides present and future behaviors and decisions. In a grant proposal, a vision statement helps to establish the *tone* of why a specific set of objectives and activities are being suggested. If the guidelines do not request the inclusion of a vision statement, then you must ask yourself, "Would a vision statement add or detract from the proposal?"

Model 1.1 can be used to judge the quality of your statements of the need or the problem.

MODEL 1.1: Evaluation of Problem or Needs Statement

Below are a series of criteria to be used in judging the needs or problem statement. Evaluate each criterion by circling the number to the right of the statement. The higher the score, the better you will have prepared your statement.

NA	=	Not Applicable
1	=	Missing
2	=	Not Readily Apparent

3	=	Somewhat Apparent					
4	=	Very Apparent					

1. Appropriate introduction is provided.		1	2	3	4
2. Logical lead to problem or needs statement.		1	2	3	4
3. Problem or need is feasible to address.		1	2	3	4
4. Statistical data support statement.	NA	1	2	3	4
5. If a training project, the "target" group has provided support to the need or problem.	NA	1	2	3	4
6. Assumptions or hypotheses are clearly stated.	NA	1	2	3	4
7. Need or problem appears to be credible.		1	2	3	4
8. Statement is clearly written.		1	2	3	4
9. The statement is presented in a logical order.		1	2	3	4
10. The vision statement is reasonable.	NA	1	2	3	4
11. What is your overall impression of statement?					

12. Strengths: _____

13. Comments for improvement: _____

PRIORITIES

This is a good spot to discuss priorities—yours and the funder's. What is a priority? A priority is a statement about the importance or merit of selected issues, actions or circumstances that you, the proposal writer, states. Often you will read a statement listing the priorities of certain courses of action. You select these statements or objectives in rank order. In some cases, you may have a list of six or seven attributes or conditions. The trick in listing priorities is to realize that they do have an order about them. To write "these seven priorities are equal" implies that you do not have a list of priorities at all. Priorities have a rank-ordering character about them and you need to address the top priority first, the secondary one and then the tertiary one. It is important as you seek systematic funding that the emphasis goes to the top priority.

Establish Priorities for Funding

Grant proposal writers may be classified into one of two groups. There are *opportunists* and there are *problem solvers*. Opportunists have the motto "If there's a dollar out there, let's go for it." These are the individuals who dash off proposals with little crafting or careful designing. They are the ones who see a chance "to get a grant" and proceed with little regard as to how the money will impact their organization. You see the point?

The problem with adopting an opportunistic view of proposal writing is that, even when funded, the infrastructure or colleagues in your organization probably will not accept the program once the grant is exhausted. Opportunists tend to act without working with those who must implement the finalized project.

Yes, we realize how tempting it is to a researcher or curriculum director to target a fast buck. But the overall impact of opportunism is to expend organizational energy on counterproductive and time-consuming projects that have no payoff for the future.

The opposite position is that of being *problem solvers*. This perspective treats the development of grant proposals as an integral part of funding activities that help an organization meet the priorities that have been established. In universities, the classic three are—teaching, research and service. More importantly, the process is democratic and open. Everyone is explicitly invited to participate in the designing of meaningful projects. Typically, a small clique writes only for themselves in organizations that adopt the opportunistic modus operandi. By having open and public work sessions, the creative juices begin to flow and a healthy interaction of ideas takes place. That is the way problems are solved. They are not solved by authoritarian dictums.

It is vitally important for key individuals in a university to discuss openly the perspective to which they subscribe. Such policy discussions help establish, if you please, a vision of why outside funding is to be solicited. Clearly, it distinguishes "good" money—i.e., money that expands the mission of the university or school—from "bad"; i.e., a project that has virtually zero impact on the institution's mission. There are always numerous funders who support just about every conceivable project.

Time is short in all organizations. Thus, it behooves administrators and non-administrators, alike, to have priority listing of what needs urgent outside funding. Such a priority helps to channel the time-consuming efforts of proposal writing to the most constructive and worthwhile uses.

The Priorities of Funders

The biggest mistake that any grant proposal writer can make is to assume that, once you have a carefully developed and crafted document, it is ready for submission. No, not yet. At this point, we suggest identifying funding sources that have priorities coinciding with yours.

Every funding agency has either explicitly written funding priorities or implicitly stated ones. Let us discuss each. After you begin the preliminary work of preparing a proposal for your number one priority, you need to examine the various reports, directories and guidelines of funders. Chapter 2 presents a rather detailed strategy on how to monitor funding sources. So, at this point, we will be general rather than specific.

Once you have a funder's report or guidelines, carefully examine its current funding priorities. If you observe that a certain business only funds proposals from Marin County, California, then do not read any further if your organization is located out of Marin County. Many foundations are geographically bound. That is, they only fund proposals that emanate from a specified geographic sector.

Funders will specify if they provide money for scholarships, basic research, capital improvements, remodeling, equipment or travel. Do pay careful attention to these explicitly stated priorities.

But let's assume you examine a guideline and it is silent about priorities. This requires some probing into one of the sources listed in Chapter 2. Do your "homework." Examine what types of projects were funded last year or in the immediate past. If you note that they did not fund any local school district, then it is a safe conclusion that they do not. Often grant-seekers assume that if a funder has never funded *my type* of proposal, then "I'll be their first to be funded." Wrong: You will not be the first because their previous funding patterns indicate your type of proposal is not being funded. You can also contact the agency office with a specific query that you were unable to find in their various reports. They will quickly tell you if they fund in that arena.

The essence of this discussion is that you have to play the probabilities of being funded. You have a higher probability of being funded if similar types of projects have been previously funded. The reverse is also valid. This line of reasoning can change if a new funding priority is established. That is one reason for carefully monitoring funding sources in a systemic manner.

In Chapter 2, we will discuss in detail how to organize your group to become more successful in finding those funding agencies that are interested in your priorities.

The basic thread of this chapter has been on how to think about developing and crafting the grant proposal. Let us now shift our orientation to some issues that are unique to funding large projects.

WRITING BIG PROPOSALS

Successful proposals for external support of institutional needs may be generated in a variety of ways. This section describes one model that may be useful when developing comprehensive improvement proposals involving several disciplines or units. Many of the suggestions may not be applicable in the preparation of smaller, more focused proposals involving one writer. However, these tips are applicable whenever you need to work with even one other who resides in a different unit.

Several important steps in proposal development should take place *before* the project plan is actually written. Careful attention to the preliminary aspects results in a more carefully crafted proposal and improves chances for funding.

Insufficient resources for meeting institutional goals and objectives often force faculty and other institutional officials to seek external support for their programs. Prior to seeking such support, a necessary step is to involve faculty and administrators who identify and prioritize significant needs among those existing at the institution. It is essential to decide whether a comprehensive improvement plan or one which focuses on a narrowly defined area can best address those needs. In searching for sources of external support, funding agency goals and objectives should be compared with those of the institution's improvement goals. A reasonable match between the two must be reflected before developing a proposal. Program guidelines should be thoroughly examined for information relating to eligibility and limitations, matching requirements, if any, and proposal deadlines.

Expanding the Circle

After an agency or foundation program has been identified as one for which a proposal might be developed, it is important to enlarge the circle of people at the institution, both faculty and administrators, who will be involved in the development of the proposal. Early involvement is necessary to determine the extent of receptivity of colleagues and administrators to the proposed plan and to gauge the specific assistance that can be expected from them. Forms of assistance might include data collection, review of research, budget and proposal preparation, review of the final proposal, and identification of specific roles for faculty in the plan. Discussions with faculty members can reveal who is interested in becoming involved in the project, in what ways, to what extent, and what relevant skills they can bring to the project.

At this point at least three local administrative procedures must be met: Determine whose approval is needed (President, Dean, Division/Department Chairperson, Curriculum Committee); how much time may be required in the approval chain; who can provide various pieces of information (e.g., Facilities and Administrative Costs—formerly called the indirect cost rate—enrollment data). In the public schools, it would be superintendent, principal, curriculum director and faculty.

Now is the time to determine whether similar proposals have been submitted by the institution in the recent past, and their final outcomes. Verbatim reviewer comments should be requested and examined to learn the reasons why previous proposals were not successful. It is also possible to request copies of successful proposals submitted to federal agency programs by other institutions of comparable size, type, location, with similar needs, problems. These can provide useful information about ideas being tried elsewhere, methods of data collection and proposal styles. A note of caution: Most foundations do not provide reviewer comments. However, federal and state agencies, on request, will send verbatim reviewer comments or a summary of them.

Four other important questions need to be considered at this stage. Have previous projects related to the one under consideration been funded at the institution? If so, is there potential duplication or overlap between them? Are others in the institution now developing improvement proposals? Is there possible duplication or overlap?

If other agencies or groups are to be involved in the project, then they must be included from the start. More than likely, compromises will be necessary relating to the scope or magnitude of the proposal. Most organizations, such as school districts, need the official endorsement of their boards of trustees. They meet usually once a month. Their support requires very careful and detailed, long-range planning. Further, if there is need for some type of inter-agency committee, that group needs to be identified and formally invited to participate.

Preparing the Concept Paper

The next major step is the development of an outline of problems and the proposed plan to solve them. We refer to this step as developing a "concept paper." You sketch out the basic concepts or priorities for which funding might be appropriate. Continued dialog and "brainstorming" with others are vital at this stage. Alternative solutions to problems should be considered. The rationale for the final solutions for which support will be requested should be carefully developed. Locally available resources that might be obtained without outside funding need to be identified. A literature search would be most appropriate to see if others have already done work in areas included in the preliminary plans e.g., development of laboratory modules, preparation of multimedia systems or computer courseware.

Preliminary costs, time estimates for project implementation, and roles for key project personnel need to be detailed at this point. Guidelines of the program to which the proposal will be submitted should be rechecked to be certain that there is a proper match. Another search for alternative or additional funding sources might also be appropriate at this point.

Supporting data and descriptions of existing programs and facilities to validate the institution's request for assistance are crucial in the proposal development process and to the proposer, per se. It is important to present clear and accurate baseline data in the proposed improvement plan. Some of the items that probably should be included are: Total institutional enrollment, enrollment in relevant courses, number of specific majors and any significant changes in recent years in each of these; a description of fields in which majors are offered and other course offerings; physical facilities, including major equipment holdings; student retention rates; student performance in standardized tests, as appropriate; number of graduates pursuing advanced degrees by disciplines, institutions; and profiles of the faculty, including total number, number in respective disciplines, types

13

of degrees held, minority representation, specific skills that are relevant to the proposed project.

Other information needed before writing the final proposal and budget include: up-to-date descriptions and costs of equipment and materials proposed for purchase; travel costs; identification of consultants; institutional rates for staff benefits, staff replacements, consultants and indirect costs—now called Facilities and Administrative (F&A) Costs. If the institution does not have an established F&A cost rate, the business office will need to contact the agency's grants and contracts office regarding the establishment of such a rate. This step would lead to the submission of organization management and financial information to qualify for indirect cost recovery. (The concept of Facilities and Administrative Costs [indirect costs] is discussed more fully in Chapter 6.)

While specific proposals may require other additional preliminary activities because of special features, for the most part you should be ready to draft a complete proposal setting forth what your institution wants to do, why and how it is to be done, who will be involved and in what ways, how success will be measured and how successful outcomes of the project will be "institutionalized."

Finalizing the Proposal

There are two additional important steps to be considered before developing the final version of the proposal. Discussions should be held with appropriate institutional officials regarding any and all implied institutional obligations during the project as well as after the project ceases. Their explicit endorsement and support in the final proposal are critical. In some funding programs, it will be necessary, as part of the proposal, to include a signed "Local Review Statement," showing formal endorsement by an appropriate institutional official. Many foundations will only accept one proposal from an institution, so be certain that yours is that one. Further, there may be need for an Institutional Review Board (IRB) statement, especially if human subjects are involved. In Chapter 7 we amplify the discussion of the IRB. In addition, the draft proposal should be reviewed by others playing key roles in the project for their concurrence on the final project plan.

Prior to the submission of the proposal, it is also advisable to ask two or more colleagues not involved in developing the proposal to review it, applying the criteria published in the agency's guidelines. When the proposal is submitted to peer review by the funding program, reviewers will use these same criteria. (Remember that reviewers will have only what is presented in the institution's proposal on which to make a judgment as to its merit.) After suggestions resulting from the colleague review have been carefully considered, the final proposal should be prepared and submitted to the agency in sufficient time to meet any established closing date.

Again, a note of caution: Time is of essence! Some federal agencies may announce a Request for Proposals (RFPs) or Request for Applications (RFAs) with as few as six weeks' lead time. Such urgency will require Herculean efforts to complete all the necessary elements for a big proposal before the deadline date and time. If your proposal requires approval from the IRB, then contact the group for an expedited review. Note: An expedited review may take as long as 10 business days. A non-expedited review could take at least one month, as most IRBs only meet once a month.

A list of key points follows. These will be useful as you're developing your proposal. The list could be used as a final checklist to make sure that there are no major omissions from the proposal. Of course, one must always remember: **Follow the published guidelines!**

CHECKLIST: Big Proposal Development

☐ RESPONSIBILITY

Recognize that, as proposed project director, you are accepting a responsibility on behalf of your colleagues, your institution and, ultimately, your students.

☐ INSTITUTIONAL NEEDS

Identify and prioritize pressing unmet institutional needs. Make sure your institution's goals and proposal objectives are compatible with those of the funding source. Don't chase dollars for dollars' sake.

☐ INSTITUTIONAL AND STAFF CAPABILITIES

Be certain that what is being proposed is something your institution can do well and that the staff available on campus can carry out the effort.

☐ PLANNING

Involve other faculty; get approval and support of the central administration and outside agencies, if needed.

☐ CHAIN OF REASONING

Repeat or maintain central ideas throughout the proposal.

☐ DATA COLLECTION

Do it early in the proposal development process; present it clearly; make sure information is up to date and accurate.

☐ POSITIVE WRITING STYLE

Avoid using "maybe," "probably," "hopefully" and "might."

☐ JARGON

Avoid it!

☐ SCOPE OF EFFORT

Make sure it is reasonable, feasible and economical.

☐ **TIMETABLE**
Make it realistic; list major project milestones.

☐ **BUDGET**
Be certain that items in the budget are discussed and justified in the narrative, and that items or positions discussed in the narrative are reflected in the budget.

☐ **KEY PROJECT PERSONNEL**
Briefly describe their responsibilities and skills relevant to the project. Append vitae.

☐ **OUTREACH**
Give evidence that ideas will be useful to others and that they are transferable.

☐ **EXPECTED OUTCOMES**
Describe what could result from the proposed effort if all goes well.

☐ **MONITORING/EVALUATION**
Show how it is planned to find out if the project is accomplishing what was intended. Describe specific plans for measuring project impact.

☐ **CONTINUATION PLANS**
Give specific evidence of your institution's commitment to continue successful components of the proposed project.

☐ **COLLEAGUE REVIEW**
Have colleagues review the proposal prior to submission using criteria published in the guidelines.

☐ **CLEARING HOUSE APPROVAL**
Obtain a state clearing house number if one is required. (Some states have governing agencies that approve or disapprove submission of a proposal.)

☐ **ENDORSEMENTS**
Append letters of endorsements from agencies or affiliated groups to show their support.

☐ **ASSURANCES**
Complete IRB assurances as needed.

☐ **MECHANICS**
Number pages, proofread, have proper signatures, assemble correctly and follow organizational instructions in the guidelines.

☐ **DEADLINES**
Send proposal via certified, receipt return mail at least five days prior to the announced deadline date, or send by guaranteed parcel delivery service or via E-mail at least two days in advance of the deadline.

Chapter 2

Monitoring Funding Sources

CHAPTER SUMMARY

- Utilizing Your Infrastructure to Locate Funding Sources
- Seeking Governmental Sources
- Foundation Resources
- Contacting the Business Sector
- A Checklist of Questions for Knowing the Funder

No question about it, there is always a sense of victory when you receive the long-awaited letter or E-mail from the granting agency and it begins, "We are pleased . . . " No need to read any further—that lead is only sent when you receive a grant award. Individuals are often funded on a routine basis by having carefully monitored the various information sources. This is a case of advance planning and opportunity converging. However, if a school, a school district, a non-profit agency or an institution of higher education wants to maximize its grant-writing efforts, then some type of organizational commitment must be made. That effort is expanded below.

UTILIZING YOUR INFRASTRUCTURE TO LOCATE FUNDING SOURCES

It must be assumed that your organization has democratically identified its funding priorities. Given that list, everyone knows what types of projects are going to be encouraged or supported. However, most institutions of higher education have some type of office or appointed individual who is the "designated grant-seeker or "development officer." This person is responsible to monitor various guides and resource indexes and inform all others of the news that is relevant to their needs.

Major universities, that is, those who are ranked as the top 100 in research or extramural funds, all have some type of helping group to inform the faculty of potential opportunities.

The key to success in such an operation is to work closely with that person who is a supporter of ideas. The individual who heads such an effort wants to work with others and is truly a reflective leader. These individuals bask in the successes that others have had in writing funded grant proposals.

This central office makes a conscious effort to alert all of funding potentials. The individuals monitor relevant federal, state, foundation and business guides. Later in this chapter, a detailed listing of selected key guides will be presented. Once the search is completed, a newsletter is usually distributed in either print form or electronically so that news and deadlines are received in a timely fashion.

Another major task for the office is to assemble writing teams that may help you prepare that winning grant. Most proposals will have more than one person involved and the writing teams help to forge commitment to implementation.

Another important task is to conduct in-service training on proposal writing and those all important factors associated with "Responsible Conduct of Research," which we will cover in a later chapter. This unit also acts as the central clearing house to expedite the processing and submitting of the required proposals.

SEEKING GOVERNMENTAL SOURCES

The number of federal government agencies awarding grants to schools, businesses, foundations, non-profit groups, universities and other public agencies is staggering: about 1,350 programs and 51 agencies. The way the Feds disseminate news about funding opportunities is through three very different sources, with each discussed below.

Catalog of Federal Domestic Assistance

The most important index available for identifying federal resources is the *Catalog of Federal Domestic Assistance* (CFDA). The CFDA is an absolute must for anyone seeking any of the 15 types of federal assistance, which contains information on 2,068 federal assistance programs, be it funds, equipment or services. This loose-leaf, 2,611-page, five-inch-thick compendium is published each year by the General Services Administration under the Office of Management and Budget. The CFDA is also on-line at www.cfda.gov. At least once each year a supplement is provided so that the programs are kept current.

What does the CFDA contain? The catalog is divided into four basic sections: (1) indices, (2) program descriptions, (3) deadlines index and (4) various appendices. As you open the cover, there are six easy-to-use indices. The first is the Agency Index Summary that describes the functions and activities of the respective federal agencies responsible for administering programs. A five-digit CFDA is assigned to every program. The CFDA two-digit prefixes are always the same for each department or agency, which helps to narrow your search. See Table 2.1 for a selected listing of the CFDA two-digit prefixes. Thus, once you know that NASA is 43 or Education is 84, you can then more easily locate specific programs by the last three digits of a five-digit number, e.g., 84.164.

The second index is the Agency Program Index that lists, in numerical order by five digits, all programs, titles, agency responsible and the kind of assistance being offered—financial, non-financial or combined.

The Functional Index Summary lists categories of support. For example, under the title "Resource Conservation and Development," a total of 34 different programs are identified by that five-digit CFDA number. Under the category of "Higher Education," 49 different programs are listed by title.

There is also an alphabetical Subject Index that provides a detailed listing of programs by various topics. Popular names, services or selected beneficiaries are all followed by that five-digit number. For example, under the subject of "Computers" are 9 topics and 14 different CFDA numbers. No question about it, the index system is designed to be user-friendly.

The second main section of the CFDA is the compilation of Program Descriptions arranged in numerical order from 10.001, "Agricultural Research-Basic and Applied," to 97.118 (2,053 pages later), "Advanced Surveillance Program Projects." These components of the CFDA provide a major piece for grant-seekers' "Toolbox." Each program is described with several items of information.

- Agency
- Authorization
- Objectives
- Types of Assistance
- Uses and Restrictions
- Credentials/Documentation
- Eligibility Requirements
- Pre-application Coordination
- Application and Award Process
- Award Procedures
- Deadlines
- Range of Approval/Disapproval Time
- Appeals
- Renewals
- Financial Information
- Assistance Consideration
- Program Accomplishments

19

Table 2.1 Selected basic two-digit prefixes used in the
Catalog of Federal Domestic Assistance

CFDA Prefix	Selected U.S. Department or Agency
10	Agriculture
11	Commerce
12	Defense
14	Housing and Urban Development
15	Interior
16	Justice
17	Labor
19	State
20	Transportation
21	Treasury
39	General Services Administration
42	Library of Congress
43	National Aeronautics and Space Administration
45	National Endowment for the Arts and Humanities
47	National Science Foundation
59	Small Business Administration
64	Veterans Affairs
66	Environment
68	National Gallery of Art
81	Energy
82	Information Agency
84	Education
85	Harry S. Truman Scholarship Foundation
89	National Archives and Records Administration
93	Health and Human Services
97	Homeland Security

- Reports
- Regulations, Guidelines and Literature
- Audits
- Information Contacts
- Related Programs
- Examples of Funded Projects
- Criteria for Selecting Proposals

Having all that information before you gives you an advantage over all others who are not aware of the CFDA. For example, the description lists the program's appropriation along with the range of previous awards and an average award. Knowing these figures, you can better gauge the scope of your intended project.

Further, if you have any questions about the program, a contact person is listed. It's recommended that you telephone these persons and ask how many awards will be funded, how many are new, how many are renewals, and what is the size of the competition. If there are only three awards nationally and the program officer expects 300 applications, the odds of being funded are 1 in 100 or a 1 percent probability. Therefore you might consider this too risky to enter. If you run fourth in this competition, you get—as they say in the rodeo business—only the applause.

And, the CFDA has so much more, such as deadlines index and several informational appendices. The CFDA is a useful federal "toolbox." You simply need to spend an hour with it. (But not curled up in your lap, it's too big for that: maybe propped open on an old door that is converted to a table.) However, your computer can be the tool by which to open a compendium of information. Once you identify the program aspects, print out the relevant pages. The on-line versions mirror-image the print editions, so print out what you need. Institutions of Higher Education (IHE) often maintain a list of individuals geared toward specific arenas.

The Federal Register

Ever use the term "red tape"? Well, the *Federal Register* (FR) *is* the red tape. The FR is published every weekday by the U.S. Government Printing Office. The FR differs from the CFDA in that it spells out all new federal rules and regulations for every federal department. It is a necessary item for your grant-seeker "toolbox," since it provides the newer versions of rules and regulations that guide all those 2,000 plus federal programs. Since you never know when programs will be announced, you need the FR. The FR provides the following:

- Presidential Orders
- Program Rules and Regulations

- Proposed Rules
- Notices of Advisory Meetings
- Program Announcements
- Requests for Application
- Deadline Dates

It's important to know the deadline dates for various programs. The Department of Education often publishes several dozen deadline dates in various issues of the FR. These deadlines are often more current than those found in the CFDA. And each program is identified by the five-digit CFDA number. So these two documents need to be used in tandem. The CFDA gives all the program details, rules and regulations affecting the program, funding information and a program officer or contact person with a telephone number.

Often new programs are first announced by "proposed rules and regulations." (Old pros call them "rules-n-regs.") Here is a real tip for you. The proposed rules 'n' regs change very little from the final ones, so once the proposed rules and regulations are available, get your teams organized and start writing. This gives you a great time advantage over the uninformed competition. Contact the identified program officer and ask for the application materials. If new ones are not yet ready, request a copy of last year's. Be proactive; that's why you should systematically monitor the CFDA and FR.

When proposed rules 'n' regs are printed, you are invited to respond. Do send the noted official your candid comments. You just may help shape the direction of the . . . red tape; that is, your comments might be incorporated in the final versions.

When notices of advisory meetings are given, and it is a program that meets your priorities, call and ask for a "summary" of the meeting. Advisory meetings for various governmental groups are held rather irregularly. These advisory groups shape the direction of specific programs. For example, The NSF advisory group on research may suggest a new area for funding. This suggestion will be printed in that group's minutes, which will be published in the FR. NB: Call the responsible program officer and ask for the summary, not the minutes. The minutes are not published until approved at a subsequent meeting. By having a summary, you know what direction the program may take. It is all part of being proactive.

Beyond information about deadlines, the FR contains the index to the *Code of Federal Regulations* (CFR). These documents contain the codified general and permanent rules that are published in the *Federal Register*. There are 50 different CFR titles which are updated quarterly. Education's code is 34. The CFR is also accessible on-line. These items are really useful to your business office.

FedBizOpps (Formerly the *Commerce Business Daily*)

The last major resource used to identify federal sources is the *FedBizOpps* (FBO). This document is published regularly, like the FR. The average person may not ever use the FBO, but if your organization is seeking to participate fully by providing goods or services to the federal government, then this is a necessity.

The federal government does not really own many businesses other than the mint and armed forces. Virtually all-governmental services are bid out to the private sector and it is a tidy $200 billion per year. This would range from scrubbing the halls of a local post office to the building of a new post office. Surprised? Most people are. To take part in the bidding process, you subscribe to the FBO, which lists all the desired government procurements, services, supplies, property sales, training, leasing, repair and expert or consultant services.

There are actually 99 codes used in the FBO by which services and supplies are classified. Nineteen different letter codes, A, H, U . . . Z, describe the types of services being requested. A few are listed below.

A   Research and Development
H   Quality Control, Testing and Inspection Service
U   Education and Training Services
Y   Transportation, Travel and Relocation Services

There are 78 two-digit codes for supplies, equipment and materials, including:

14   Guided Missiles
48   Valves
69   Training Aids and Devices
76   Books, Maps and Other Publications

By reviewing the respective alphabet codes, which can be purchased separately, in each issue you find what the federal government wants. You then contact the person listed and request an RFP or Request for Proposal. By mail or electronically, you will receive a printed description of what the government requires and how offers will be evaluated. You send in your bid, following carefully the conditions set in the RFP. Typically, the top contenders are requested to renegotiate the contract. Finally, an award is given based on a combination of the lowest price and technical merit of the bidders. The FBO also lists the winners of awards in each issue.

As was mentioned earlier, most schools do not compete in this arena because they simply do not know about the FBO. This is a great source for obtaining complimentary governmental excess equipment, for example, computers, printers and the like. By examining the FBO, we have helped school districts obtain surplus government computers that were brand new. Various items of scientific equipment are listed and there is usually no cost to obtaining them.

FOUNDATION RESOURCES

There is one federal government, 50 state governments, and currently 120,810 different foundations with 88,000 being active. Collectively, the total assets are over $566 billion! You don't have to use "modern math" to realize that the private sector plays a major role in public philanthropy. It is rather easy to apply for funding, but you really have to do a good deal of "homework" before you dash off that letter seeking foundation support. Actually, the strategies suggested in searching federal grants are almost identical when seeking potential foundation donors.

Recall, your first step to "check out the feds" was the *Catalog of Federal Domestic Assistance* (CFDA). Similar resources are available by which to examine foundation-funding priorities. A good fast start is the *Foundation 1,000*. This 3,030-page tome provides a detailed listing of the 1,000 largest foundations in the United States. These large foundations contribute almost two-thirds of the yearly donations made. How do you use this resource? Currently the print edition is not available. Instead, you buy a subscription on-line for $195 to $1,295 per year, depending on the type and amount of information you want. Most university libraries have the print or on-line versions of foundation resources.

Check the index. An excellent index is included so that your specific subject area can be identified. Once you find a potential funder, you should study the pattern of gifts that have been made. In most cases, the profiles will show current funding priorities, geographic or spending limitations, key foundation officers, assets and description of recently funded groups. You need to examine all the information given in the profile so that you select exactly the right foundation.

As you examine previous gifts, look for those with similar purposes to what you are pursuing. For example, you might want scholarship support for deserving students. If you notice that no scholarship support is listed in the profile, act no further. Do not delude yourself that you can make such a grand case that your organization will be the first. Foundations change their funding patterns only when they modify their announced *funding priorities*. And in cases where the founder of the trust has specified rigid limitations, they may not.

There are several excellent source books now available to grant-seekers that present foundation profiles. An annotated listing is located in Appendix B of this book as a "toolbox" for grant-seekers. Among the many informative volumes now available, we shall list but three that tend to cover the field. The 45th edition of the *Annual Register of Grant Support: A Directory of Funding Sources* provides a comprehensive list of 3,200 North American grant-making organizations. Included are foundations, businesses, unions, governmental agencies, professional associations and others. Rather detailed summaries are provided about each entry. After examining the index and studying the summary, you can make a decision about whether to initiate contact with potential funders. This 1,220-page directory

24

(costing $269.00) will be a checkpoint against other directories as you follow a specific foundation, and is also on-line.

The Foundation Directory, 2011 edition, lists 100,000 entries on 2,860 pages and is limited to those foundations making awards of at least $200,000 yearly and having $2 million in assets. This source is helpful in cross-checking a foundation to be certain that it makes large enough contributions. Or, if you seek a gift in excess of $200,000, you'll know *not* to approach this group. This directory costs $215.00.

Finally, there is the *Guide to U.S. Foundations, Their Trustees, Officers, and Donors*. This guide has 37,211 entries, has 8,491 pages and includes 74,000 foundations and was last published in 2007. This guide, which is now available on-line through the Foundation Center, has a compilation of all state and local foundation directories. The costs vary by services required. Knowing how to access all the foundations in your state can be most helpful as you plan a long-range funding plan. We will discuss this further later.

Contacting Foundations

You want to avoid using identical "form letters" when contacting foundations or businesses for grants. This is *not* the way to approach businesses or foundations. Form letters are discarded without reply. You should carefully match your funding needs with the funding priorities of the foundation. Once you have the list narrowed to those having the highest probabilities of funding your proposal, you write a specific letter of inquiry to that organization.

You introduce your organization, explain its goal, how it fits the apparent priorities of the foundation, that you have an IRS 501 (c) (3) or IRS 501 (c) (5) non-profit designation, and that you would like to submit a full proposal. All of this is done on one page. The reason for brevity is that the vast bulk of foundations do not have any paid staff members to process correspondence. Most have only one person at the office. Thousands have no paid staff members. If you cannot state your query in one page, it probably won't be read either.

We mentioned IRS 501 (c) (3) and IRS 501 (c) (5). What are they? The Federal Internal Revenue Service officially designates all non-profit organizations in the United States. In order for you to receive any foundation money, your group must be legally described as a non-profit organization. The very least is to be declared a state non-profit organization. The Secretary of State at the Capitol can send you the necessary forms to incorporate as a non-profit group. This is usually the first step to gaining an IRS designation. Recall the emphasis above is on "group" or "organization." The reason for the explicitness is that foundations rarely fund individuals. Yes, the John D. and Catherine T. MacArthur Foundation has made the day for scores of persons who were judged as being among the nation's most talented or creative individuals. But, in the main, foundations fund organizations. This obviously precludes scholarships, travel grants or honors.

Once you contact a person at the foundation and obtain either their funding priorities or their guidelines, the rest is up to you. For the most part, foundations use a two-phase application process. In phase one, they suggest sending a short summary or abstract of the proposed project. Typically, this one- or two-page piece contains (1) need or problem and significance, (2) goals and objectives, (3) procedures or methodology, (4) evaluation model, (5) personnel, (6) short budget note and (7) IRS 501 (c) (3) letter. These components will be thoroughly discussed in Chapters 3–6 respectively. With the advent of on-line submissions, many foundations provide an electronic blueprint to be followed exactly—even specifying how many "characters" you may print in the statement.

The acceptance rate of the initial phase "applications" is usually low. In some cases, they are declined at a rate of 98 percent or even greater. That is, most applicants in the phase one submission process are not encouraged to make a full application in phase two.

Assuming you do receive an invitation to phase two, you will be asked to submit a full proposal. A page limitation will be the norm, usually about 10 to 15 pages total. The phase two application format requires amplification of the six key points noted above. Several foundations require phase two applications that do not exceed two pages! At phase two, you have rather favorable odds of being funded. The range is from 50 to 100 percent. A similar two-phase approach is also used by several federal agencies, e.g., the National Science Foundation (NSF). the Fund for the Improvement of Post-Secondary Education (FIPSE), CFDA Number 84.116 no longer uses a two-step process, although it has in the past. However, many U.S. Department of Education competitions still use a two-phase approach. Check the CFDA for details.

As was implied earlier, the bulk of those 75,000 charitable foundations are "mom 'n' pop" organizations. That term is not used pejoratively, but to describe their modus operandi. Keep in mind many of the smaller foundations tend to be under-utilized as far as receiving proposals. By doing your homework, you just might locate a small foundation that funds exactly what you need. If you can, contact the founders or benefactors personally—so much the better. Foundation funders like to know whom they are supporting. Funding decisions have been known to be made from "the heart."

In some cases, you may have a project that is too large for smaller foundations and yet not in the funding priority of larger ones. In this case, you subdivide the project by some logical means and you contact different foundations with one aspect of the full project. But you do need to inform each foundation how you are subdividing the project, who is being contacted and for what. Honesty is an absolute must in this business.

One question that is frequently asked is, "May I submit the same proposal to different foundations?" Our answer is always "No!" It is not ethical to submit simultaneous applications of the same proposal to different foundations.

Funders often compare notes on formal or informal bases. Once the people involved in philanthropy realize that you are simple "mooching," your reputation will precede you.

Again, successful foundation grant-seekers spend hours examining annual reports, statements and even the IRS 990-PF forms to determine the best probability for funding. The IRS 990-PF forms are those submitted each year by all foundations. Every grant that is awarded is listed in this handy form. You can obtain a copy of any foundation's fiscal report by contacting a field office of the Internal Revenue Service or by contacting any public library that has been designated as a "funding center." The Foundation Center of New York City designates selected libraries in the United States as Foundation Center Libraries and each local center has a wealth of bibliographic information, plus most of the reference books that you'll ever need to identify a potential funder. The sites are listed in the *Foundation Directory* and may be found on-line at http://foundation center.org/collections.

When contacting state or local foundations, you should follow the same procedures. Forty-three states publish very detailed foundation directories. For a complete listing of state and local foundation directories, go to http://foundation center.org/getstarted/topical/sl-dir.html.

What about contacting businesses—what strategy do you employ? Let us discuss that next.

CONTACTING THE BUSINESS SECTOR

"Businesses tend to fund in the shadow of their 'smokestacks'." That little truism sums up the status of business funding. It is often tempting to write a letter requesting assistance from some large corporation or business. But, they tend to link philanthropy with public relations. If Hewlett-Packard has a major plant in your town or county, then you might contact them.

Typically, you initiate a contact with the firm's public relations office. If they have a separate philanthropic office, it will be conveyed through public relations. Businesses operate very similarly to foundations. Most require a two-phase application. There are over 1,900 businesses and corporations who fund a company foundation. For example, the Weyerhaeuser Company funds its own Weyerhaeuser Company Foundation. The International Paper Company likewise. The key to corporate giving is their annual profit and loss statement. If business is brisk and profits are growing, then corporate funding to their respective foundations or public relations offices increases. So, before you write that carefully crafted letter to the Exxon Corporation, check their most recent annual report. If profits are up, send the request. If profits are down, you might seek others.

As with foundations, businesses and corporations like to know the recipients of their generosity. Any potential meeting of the "right person" in the corporate structure is helpful. Many companies have a formal application process. Others tend to be more informal. For the latter, use the generic model being described in this book.

One last point—funders usually meet once, twice or four times each year to evaluate grant proposals. It is important to find out what months the selection committee meets. In that manner, you can time the arrival of your letter or full proposal to arrive for the pending meeting. If you miss one deadline, you have to wait until the next to find out how you fared. And please do not telephone the company to ask about the status of your proposal! They will notify you.

A key resource to identify potential private sector funders is the 17th edition of the *National Directory of Corporate Giving*. Over 4,400 company profiles are cataloged with their programs of interest being listed and costs $195.00.

By subscribing to one of the various weekly grant services, e.g., *Education Grants Alert* ($305 per year), those of you in the K-12 sector will be given numerous tips about corporate funding sources for 38 weeks.

Contacting foundations and businesses is an art form. Do keep in mind that the emphasis in this book is grant proposal writing. It is not fundraising. Fundraising is an entirely different arena that we will delimit. And, yes, remember these funders have all been successful in some line of work. They did not become financially successful by taking unnecessary risks. As you craft your letter or proposal, work in the message that what you are suggesting is a practical and successful idea. Few, if any, businesses, corporations or foundations will fund some risky-sounding adventure.

There are some questions you need to ask about all potential funders to help you frame those items. Let us close this chapter with a detailed checklist of questions that you need to know about your potential funder.

CHECKLIST: Questions for Knowing the Funder

1. Does the funder allocate funds on some established priority?

2. How many dollars does the funder have available to award for project activity this year? How does this figure compare to the figure for previous years, including last year?

3. What is the average size of a grant or contract that has been authorized for the prior year of the funder? Can you obtain a list of these awards, including project title, principal investigator and address? Is there a maximum amount that can be awarded to any one recipient?

4. Does the funder consider itself in the *seed-money* area of project support, or does it make it a policy to continue with project support if promising results are obtained? If so, how much of the current year's funds is earmarked for the continuation of existing projects and how much is to help initiate new projects?

5. Does the funder conduct a preliminary screening of proposal concepts based on a letter of *intent to submit* before actually giving the go-ahead to submit a full proposal?

6. Does the funder have guidelines prepared for use by organizations in preparing proposals? If not, does the funder have a set of regulations that are used *internally* in the administration of project grants? If not, and the funder is a state or federal agency, can they supply you with a copy of specific legislation under which the funding program is authorized?

7. Does the funder seek to allocate or award project funds on the basis of geographic location of the recipients?

8. What restrictions apply to project funds? Does the funder provide for Facilities and Administrative Costs (aka indirect costs)?

9. Are projects budgeted so that the awarded funds cover all of the direct costs of doing projects? Are you required to put up some percentage of *matching* funds at the local level? If so, can the matching amount be *in-kind* costs on the part of your own organization or must they be in cash?

10. In the case of projects that involve the development of a *product*, e.g., an instrument, a book, a computer program, a set of instructional materials, who retains the rights to the material? Who can copyright the material?

11. Does the funder have a deadline for the receipt of applications or proposals for funding?

12. Can you obtain a copy of a previously successful proposal or contract that has been funded?

Chapter 3

Establishing Needs

CHAPTER SUMMARY

- Conducting Needs Assessments
- Using Surveys
- The Delphi Technique
- Focus Groups
- Conclusion
- Checklist for Needs Assessments

A significant proportion of funded projects relate to staff development, program development or the offering of a service. To prepare a successful proposal to fund these activities or other similar ones, you are generally required to show a "need" or gather objective data that show a need. These are accomplished by conducting some type of needs assessment. Needs-driven projects are based on clearly defined criteria.

Preparing successful needs assessments combines the art of sensing what requires improvement and the science of collecting accurate data by which to base predictions. Thus, needs assessments depend on planning, on determining what data to collect and on providing decision-makers with coherent statements spelling out well-identified areas requiring new or continued fiscal or material support. Before requesting additional resources, it is most important to identify the existing human resources in the organization. Untapped human resources should be marshaled to remedy identified problems or needs. And, since the typical state and federal grant proposals require a needs assessment to justify the funding, you must learn to prepare them effectively and persuasively. The "tips" described in this chapter are tested techniques from funded grants that can be adapted to any specific grant proposal.

CONDUCTING NEEDS ASSESSMENTS

There are many methods by which to assess needs. A few selected techniques in the process that are germane to most funding agencies or foundations are listed below:

- Testimonials from Knowledgeable Individuals
- Committee Reports
- Planning Documents
- Reviews of Literature
- Statements from Professional or Scientific Societies

While the above five techniques are far from all-inclusive and somewhat self-explanatory, this chapter will highlight the following techniques:

- Scores on Objectives or Standardized Tests
- Surveys
- Discrepancy Models
- Delphi Technique
- Focus Groups

These general methods are highlighted because they tend to be those most easily and widely used by school districts or universities (IHEs) as well as those most economical to conduct and interpret.

A *need* may be defined as some condition that requires attention, or some desire or value that is not present or not being met. In many cases, needs are simply what someone or some group "wants." Educational needs tend to arise from changing conditions or circumstances and they are discovered as "needs" relatively late.

The identification of needs is an essential element in planning for and in involving the community in educational goal setting. A *needs assessment* is a method of discovering gaps between what "is" and what "ought" to take place in the schools. Keep in mind, you must establish evidence that what you propose in a grant application is needed to improve the current condition. The difference between reality and desire is frequently referred to as a "discrepancy."

Needs assessments are conducted and needs are identified for the following reasons.

1. To discover strengths of programs or personnel.
2. To identify perceived weaknesses in programs or personnel.
3. To determine discrepancies in programs or curricula.
4. To identify "unmet" concerns.

5. To assist curriculum development through evaluation.
6. To set priorities for future or immediate actions.
7. To illustrate a novel local want.
8. To justify renewal of special areas.
9. To provide for community consensus.
10. To share the general decision-making among various constituencies.

When conducting a needs assessment, you must determine what client group will be the recipient of the intended service and if there will be intermediate groups participating as well. The responses from these individuals and their respective groups will then be summarized and included in your data set. Speaking of data, one good use for those often used, but ignored, standardized tests is to establish a need in some specific area. Let us briefly introduce using test data to establish needs and then progress to several other means.

USING SURVEYS

The typical needs assessment is usually a short questionnaire distributed to all appropriate personnel in the organization. It may contain open-ended and forced-response items. Both techniques will be discussed here after a short statement about advantages and disadvantages of surveys.

General Advantages of Questionnaires

If surveys are used, then multiple sets of needs questionnaires must be administered to subgroups. Such a method approaches a marketing concept for determining concerns and for providing successful programs. It is important that decision-makers carefully examine the relative advantages and disadvantages of forced-response questionnaires in determining apparent needs.

The following list summarizes the overall general advantages of using a questionnaire to collect needs data.

1. Many individuals can be contacted at the same time, usually through the IHE's or school district's mail service or electronically.
2. A questionnaire is less expensive to administer than a personal interview.
3. Each selected subgroup respondent receives identical questions.
4. A written questionnaire provides a vehicle for expression without fear of embarrassment to the respondent.
5. Responses are easily tabulated, depending on the design of the instrument.
6. Uniform data are gathered that allow for long-range research implications and for program development.

The above advantages must be carefully analyzed for each needs survey. Further, the timing of a survey is critical. The months of September, December, January, May and June are very poor times in which to distribute questionnaires. During these months, faculty are just gearing up or may be on vacation periods. The latter months of a school year faculty are wrapping up their courses. The summer months of July and August are totally inappropriate for mailing questionnaires to K-12 school personnel, since they are on vacation. In addition, may school districts, for example, have policies specifying that no one in the district be obliged to complete a questionnaire not officially approved by the district.

Disadvantages of a Needs Questionnaire

For every advantage of a forced-response questionnaire survey, there is an accompanying disadvantage. A summary of disadvantages includes the following:

1. The investigator is prevented from learning the respondent's motivation for answering questions.
2. Respondents may be somewhat limited in providing free expression of opinions, owing to instrument design.
3. Usually, not all questionnaires are returned.
4. Complex designs cause poor responses, or no response at all.
5. A question may have different meanings to different people.
6. Selections of the sample, per se, may cause biased results; that is, the sample may not be representative of the population.
7. Respondents may not complete the entire questionnaire.

Open-Ended Questions

An open-ended question typically does not include predetermined or forced-response categories, and the respondents are therefore free to answer in any manner desired. There are at least five reasons for asking an open-ended question: (1) to probe an idea further, (2) to accommodate categories that are incomplete or inadequate in a forced-response list, (3) to provide projective situations, (4) to generate items for forced-response surveys and (5) to elicit items for a Delphi Technique. Open-ended questions are inappropriate when forced-response categories are needed to clarify specific points.

Tabulating, quantifying results and determining meaningful generalizations tend to be more difficult when using open-ended questions. These questions require a more complex and more subjective coding system than do forced-response questions. Tabulating open-ended results involves examining each respondent's answers on an individual basis. Categories for some characteristic of the responses must also be developed, and each of the open-ended responses is then classified into one of the appropriate categories. In contrast, the categories for classifying forced-response questions are already developed by virtue of the response patterns provided by the respondents. In some cases, the investigator can combine both types of questions.

Open-ended questions can identify topics that a staff-development committee might not have generated. Thus, respondents identify needs, problems or concerns that can later be translated into forced-response questions. Open-ended questions can be asked in either personal or telephone interviews or in mailed or electronic surveys. Model 3.1 shows several different examples of open-ended questions that address "needs."

MODEL 3.1: Examples of Open-Ended Questions

When Addressing Teacher In-Service

1. What problems does this school (or district) have in teaching writing?
2. How do these problems affect you?
3. What can be done and who can solve the identified problem?

When Addressing Curriculum Needs

4. What is our most pressing curriculum need in (a) elementary schools, (b) middle schools, (c) high schools?
5. What do you think contributed to these problems?
6. What can be done and who can solve the identified problems?

When Addressing Organizational Needs

7. What policies or procedures are most in need of change to improve the schools?
8. How do these policies or procedures affect the way in which you do your job?
9. Who could solve these problems?

Forced-Response Questions

As the term implies, in this question type a respondent can logically select only one category because the responses are already established and are mutually exclusive. To avoid bias, the question presents an equal number of positive and negative choices. The item should be clearly stated and written as a positive statement. If negative statements are used, respondents quickly become confused.

Rensis Likert developed one of the more commonly used response continua. Note how the following examples use his response patterns; any of these could be used in needs assessments.

More writing experiences are needed in the middle school curriculum.

- ☐ Strongly Agree
- ☐ Agree
- ☐ Neither Agree nor Disagree
- ☐ Disagree
- ☐ Strongly Disagree

I would encourage the school board to promote programs aimed at providing job skills for the physically and academically challenged.

- ☐ Encourage Very Much
- ☐ Encourage
- ☐ No Opinion
- ☐ Discourage
- ☐ Discourage Very Much

How well do you like attending workshops as compared to other instructional procedures?

- ☐ I like workshops much better.
- ☐ I like workshops a little better.
- ☐ I like all instructional procedures about equally well.
- ☐ I like other instructional procedures a little better than workshops.
- ☐ I like other instructional procedures much better than workshops.

The respondent is requested to select only one category of a Likert-scale item. The categories must be exhaustive and mutually exclusive. These models, as well as other models used here, are provided for your use; feel free to adapt them as you prepare items for needs assessment you conduct.

Model 3.2 shows a needs survey originally developed by David R. Stronck, which co-author Orlich later adapted. As a demonstration of a need for a revised elementary science program in a very large K-12 school district, the instrument shown here was administered to over 400 elementary schoolteachers. Data were tabulated and graphic illustrations were prepared for each item. The results were then summarized and appended to a grant application to the National Science Foundation, and subsequently the project was awarded several thousands of dollars. The needs for that grant were so well documented that the proposal reviewers rated the project higher than one might have expected.

Observe that Model 3.2 requests three types of information: (1) policy statements, (2) factual statements and (3) personal judgments. These elements typical are used in any needs assessment to justify a grant.

While Model 3.2 was designed for a grant proposal, it has subsequently been used to determine teachers' perceptions of teaching science as well as other specific subjects. It can easily be adapted to other subjects by dropping the word "science" and substituting some other subject; note how the model questions can easily be generalized and applied to IHEs.

MODEL 3.2: Elementary Science Needs Survey

Please indicate the grade level(s) in which you teach science classes _____.
On the scale at the right, please circle the number that best describes the intensity of your reaction to each of the questions.

	1 = Strongly Disagree				6 = Strongly Agree

1. Children in my school enjoy science. — 1 2 3 4 5 6

2. My school has excellent materials for scientific activities. — 1 2 3 4 5 6

3. Children in my school would like more hands-on activities in science. — 1 2 3 4 5 6

4. Our school district should adopt an activity-centered science program. — 1 2 3 4 5 6

5. My school has excellent texts for studying science. — 1 2 3 4 5 6

6. Our school district should adopt a textbook-oriented science program at my grade level. — 1 2 3 4 5 6

7. My preparation in science courses is strong. — 1 2 3 4 5 6

8. My preparation in science methods courses is strong. — 1 2 3 4 5 6

9. An in-service training program for teachers should be provided when the district is adopting a new science program. — 1 2 3 4 5 6

10. If an intensive in-service program could be provided during the summer, I would be interested in attending. — 1 2 3 4 5 6

11. Our school district should establish a system for maintaining and distributing living and consumable materials, which are used in elementary-science instruction. — 1 2 3 4 5 6

Please place any other comments on the reverse side.

NB: As shown, the items are only end-anchored. That means that only numbers 6 and 1 are explicitly described. To anchor all items, a descriptor should be included, e.g., Disagree = 2; Moderately Disagree = 3; Moderately Agree = 4; Agree = 5.

Rank-Ordered Items

When there is a need to establish some priority across your institution's needs, then a rank-ordered set of items helps focus a need. For example, some grant proposal competitions have a fixed limit, say $15,000. In this case, you want to identify those priority areas within your institution that can have a well-designed and quality program or in-service offering for that amount. Where there are limits of an award, it is imperative to apply for funding for your top priority and number one area of needs. By comparing the various subgroups of participants, you could quickly evaluate the key or top priority where the funds would be most prudently invested.

See Model 3.3 for an example of the rank-ordering technique. It should be recognized that the items being ranked would be selected by some committee or perhaps a focus group.

MODEL 3.3: Rank-Ordered Items Technique

Below is a list of in-service items. Please rank these items from 1 to 9. No. 1 has the highest priority, No. 2 is the second highest, and so on, with No. 9 the lowest priority. These items are submitted to you so that the school district staff development task force can plan for the next year.

Rank

_____ A. District-wide workshops conducted to give awareness about the NCTM [National Council of Teachers of Mathematics] Standards.

_____ B. In-service programs organized for selected teachers on teaching of mathematics problem-solving.

_____ C. In-service programs to implement the district's new mathematics manipulative program.

_____ D. Released time allowed for work on mathematics curriculum development.

_____ E. Gifted-student program mathematics models for the middle school.

_____ F. Pilot-test graphing calculators to be introduced in mathematics classes.

_____ G. Questioning strategies workshop for math teachers at all levels.

_____ H. Small-group tutorial techniques emphasizing mathematics.

_____ I. Cooperative learning techniques for math classes.

A Discrepancy Model

Needs assessment designers often use a *discrepancy analysis* as an alternative technique. A discrepancy exists when respondents perceive that "what ought to take place" is different from "what seems to take place" or "what is." In Model 3.3, the issue being addressed concerns a mathematics program. If you wanted to convert this to a discrepancy model, you could request two distinct sets of responses. The first concerns present practices; the second reflects the desired or ideal conditions. Where discrepancies are observed between these conditions, a need exists. Model 3.4 is an example of a discrepancy model.

The scoring of the items is done by averaging each response alone. If item one "what is," has an average of 3.0, and "what ought to be" is also 3.0, the difference is zero. That reveals that there's no discrepancy for that item, and the need is being met. However, in that case, if "what is" were 1.0 and "ought" were 4.0, then the maximum discrepancy of -3.0 is present: That is a negative 3.0. This is clearly a pressing need. Of course, if "what is" were 4.0 and "ought" were 1.0, then there would be a positive value of 3.0. This condition is being over-met! One could even conclude that too much emphasis is being placed on that specific item.

MODEL 3.4: Discrepancy Model Needs Assessment: In-Service Questionnaire

Please respond twice for each statement listed in the center. In the left column, labeled "What Is," circle the number that indicates your perception of the current circumstances in your school or district. Then circle one number in the right column, "What Ought to Be."

> 1 = I strongly disagree
> 2 = I disagree
> 3 = I agree
> 4 = I strongly agree

What Is	Statement	What Ought to Be
1 2 3 4	1. Teachers are offered district-wide awareness workshops about NCTM Standards.	1 2 3 4
1 2 3 4	2. In-service programs are set up for selected teachers on the teaching of mathematics problem-solving.	1 2 3 4
1 2 3 4	3. Staff programs are offered to implement the district's new mathematics manipulative program.	1 2 3 4

1 2 3 4	**4.** Teachers need a pilot project to introduce graphing calculators in mathematics classes.	1 2 3 4
1 2 3 4	**5.** Small-group tutorial techniques are used emphasizing mathematics.	1 2 3 4
1 2 3 4	**6.** Cooperative learning techniques are used in mathematics classes.	1 2 3 4

According to Thomas F. Kelly (1991), one of the architects of the Effective Schools Consortia, organizational improvement cannot happen on a systematic basis without good measurement or assessment. Kelly asserts that the most effective form of assessment is self-assessment. That is why site-based management is built into the New York Program.

Kelly notes that most needs assessment instruments are not needs assessment instruments at all. A need is defined as the difference between "what is" and "what should be" (noting a discrepancy). Kelly found that most needs assessment instruments have only one response scale for scoring. If a questionnaire were to ask one to agree or disagree if "teachers should use graphing calculators," does this establish need? Or is it just an opinion or perception of the stated question? The improper use of assessment instruments makes it nearly impossible to focus on what is truly needed and to prioritize those needs. If a change in the system has been deemed necessary, it should be justified by clear data. This rids the system of personal opinions and emphasizes the data being collected and interpreted. An example of Kelly's basic discrepancy model as shown in Model 3.5.

MODEL 3.5: Kelly's Discrepancy Model

Please answer the two questions relating to "importance" and "existence" about each statement. Responses should be based on perceptions that come from personal experiences.

Importance. From your professional viewpoint, how important is this statement in the education of students in your school? In Column A, indicate the *degree of importance* by circling one response in the five-point scale as follows:

1. Not Important
2. Somewhat Important
3. Important
4. Very Important
5. Priority

39

Existence. At what level of frequency does the condition as stated exist in your school? In Column B, indicate the existence by circling one response in the five-point scale as follows:

1. Never
2. Rare
3. Sometimes
4. Usually
5. Always

Questions	Importance	Existence
1. The mathematics curriculum is defined in terms of outcomes.	1 2 3 4 5	1 2 3 4 5
2. The mathematics outcomes, curriculum and materials are congruent.	1 2 3 4 5	1 2 3 4 5
3. The mathematics curriculum is sequential.	1 2 3 4 5	1 2 3 4 5
4. The mathematics curriculum provides repetition for learning not demonstrated.	1 2 3 4 5	1 2 3 4 5

Each of the above questions is rated for importance and existence. All data are tabulated and mean values for importance and existence are calculated for each question and for each category. If the mean value resulting from the subtraction of importance from existence is negative, then a discrepancy exists at that point. If the value is positive, then there is no discrepancy. Discrepancy values are ordered from most discrepant to least discrepant. This makes it visually easy to identify which category or criterion has a greater need than another.

THE DELPHI TECHNIQUE

The preceding sections emphasized the basics of needs assessment construction: communication, prevision, objectivity, simplicity and clarity. The designs of the instruments just discussed are rather traditional. There are, however, other information-gathering techniques that may be of value as alternative models for, or as components of, a needs assessment. The Delphi Technique has emerged as an excellent method of determining valued or desirable requirements that are lacking in the schools.

The Delphi Technique was developed and popularized by the RAND Corporation (Helmer 1967). RAND originated the system, as a method of identifying group opinions, initially about defense needs, and named it Delphi after the great oracle of Apollo. Basically, the respondents participate in three or more rounds of needs surveying, in which they receive their own data and the data for the entire group prior to each round. Delphi provides a continuous feedback system to all participants, but through a privileged design. That is, each respondent knows how he or she has responded, but does not know how any other individual responded. As such, the Delphi Technique (1) allows professional judgments to be made, (2) avoids personality conflicts and interpersonal politics and (3) reduces the possibility of high-position people forcing judgments in group discussions for the direction they deem desirable. The Delphi Technique is one means of identifying organizational consensus, determining problem areas and establishing priorities by providing detailed feedback and systematic follow-up.

One of the problems in making decisions is predicting what the future will hold. It may, therefore, be prudent to establish priorities for goals that have already been identified through other needs assessments, opinionnaires or small-group task techniques. To this end, the Delphi Technique provides a methodology for organizing and prioritizing the collective judgments of the polled group, or of those who are concerned with planning and crafting a grant proposal.

In the Delphi Technique, the initial procedure is to prepare and distribute a series of questions or problem statements for evaluation. For example, a grant proposal planner might distribute a questionnaire that contains a series of problems, statements, opinions, activities, predictions of future probabilities. In the first round, respondents provide a rank ordering, a priority or an evaluation of each item. One modification of this first step is to prepare a general statement that elicits specific responses that can ultimately be converted to items for judging.

All selected participants then receive a second list of items and are asked to either rate the list by selected criteria or reevaluate their original list in reaction to the responses of others provided in the initial ranking. Depending on the method used in the initial round, the lists are returned to each respondent with detailed group rankings plus adverse comments, new ideas for consideration and minority reports. Typically, the group mean or mode per item is computed and fed back to all participants.

The tabulator of the instruments (a list of rankings, in this case) reanalyzes the data and prepares yet a third instrument for distribution to the selected sample. This procedure continues through at least four rankings. By working with multiple submissions of the same set of data, each respondent reaffirms original opinions, modifies some or adds additional needs to the list. The technique aids in forming a clearly defined convergence pattern of major needs, plus a well-outlined minority opinion.

The Delphi Technique is easily adaptable to needs assessment surveys designed to analyze the desirability of innovative programs or projects and to justify the need for a grant proposal. A series of needs, for example, might be rated as to their significance. In addition, all respondents are encouraged to provide statements about the impact that the programs might have if instituted. For example, the

Delphi Technique is most effective when initially determining whether a group can identify issues, concerns, problems or suggested courses of action.

Another organizational problem—the formulation of educational policies and plans that allow for alternative future options—can be solved by Delphi analyses. In such cases, a task force can write preference statements. The list can then be distributed to the selected subgroup for their initial responses. The complete Delphi Technique then follows. Consensus can easily be identified for those items that have higher or lower means or modes.

In summary, the Delphi Technique is a widely used feedback mechanism by which selected members of an organization have an effect in shaping organizational goals and policies. It is a very systematic method, nevertheless, and provides yet another technique of obtaining data for the needs section of a grant proposal.

FOCUS GROUPS

The final needs assessment technique that we'll examine is one that has been adapted from market research, the old tool of business entrepreneurs. In reality, focus groups are essentially group interviews where the dynamics of group interaction help stimulate creative responses to problems or issues being resolved. Focus groups are neither formed to solve a problem nor to arrive at a consensus on some topic. The goal is to stimulate discussion and generate a wide spectrum of needs.

Typically, individuals are selected who have some characteristic in common for the topic being presented. To continue using the mathematics needs example, such a group would have a range of math teachers, other teachers, persons who apply math, and perhaps a math professor.

The focus group leaders should have experience working with groups of from six to eight. Only a few open-ended questions are presented to create the stimulus for the group discussion. The technique has proven to be excellent in clarifying issues; providing ideas, perceptions and assessments; identifying specific problems or needs; and providing feedback rather quickly.

The group leader may tape the discussions or use a recorder who lists key points made by participants to the specific questions. When no additional helpful data come forth, the group is thanked—a session usually lasts between one and three hours. Then the work begins for the leader and recorder. They must analyze the results along at least four lines: (1) findings, (2) interpretations, (3) value of findings and (4) recommendations.

The needs assessment is then summarized and presented to the proposal writing team. Focus groups can be used to initiate other forms of needs assessment or to corroborate other data.

CONCLUSION

You might be thinking to yourself, "All I wanted was a few pointers on how to construct the needs section of a grant proposal and I got the whole course on the topic." Well, not really. The needs assessment and needs section sets the stage for your proposal. A strong data-driven needs statement will hold the reviewers' attention and, when you show the significance of the project to some targeted group, you may just have the reviewers leaning toward your corner. Of course, you skillfully craft and develop the remaining sections.

One last note for those of you in IHEs: The current federal priority for Science, Technology, Engineering and Mathematics (STEM) projects appears to have a long-term priority for funding. To obtain grants for STEM projects, IHEs must collaborate with K-12 schools. However, a needs assessment must be conducted with the school partners to show the need for the STEM project and that need is supported with data gathered from the recipient groups. Again, this shows the requirement for long-range planning to meet those deadline dates.

CHECKLIST: Needs Assessment

- [ ] Information on needs is collected systematically.
- [ ] Needs assessments are keyed to specific groups within the organization.
- [ ] Local resources are assessed.
- [ ] Student outcomes are examined critically to determine specific priorities for in-service projects.
- [ ] Delphi or similar techniques are used to arrive at a consensus when prioritizing projects.
- [ ] Discrepancy analyses are used to judge needs.
- [ ] Appropriate literature is reviewed that relates to anticipated projects.
- [ ] Needs assessments lead to programs for targeted groups.
- [ ] The significance of the project is explicitly stated.

Chapter 4

Beginning Elements of the Proposal

CHAPTER SUMMARY

- Guidelines
- Objectives
- Conducting a Literature Search for Grant Proposals
- A Summary as a Working Blueprint
- Introduction/Problem/Objectives Checklist
- Evaluation Checklist for Project Abstracts or Summaries

You now have a firm grasp of what you want funded. Among your stored documents are the needs statements, basic problem, the names of one or two highly probable funders and an evaluation of support from your team members and significant administrator. You might even be that administrator. So it is time to begin the critical developing and constructing of the proposal. The first thing we do at this point is to bring out the guidelines that are specific to that respective grant and examine them in detail.

GUIDELINES

The guidelines vary from "none" for smaller foundations to a massive packet for the National Institutes of Health or the Department of Agriculture. Agencies and foundations issue guidelines to bring organizational uniformity to all applications. You should be thoroughly knowledgeable of them. It can be useful to take out a highlighter pen and physically highlight every important element. What are some of these?

Federal Guidelines

For the most part, a set of guidelines provides the blueprint that you must follow in the preparation of the full proposal or pre-proposal, as the case may be. Shown below is a listing from the guidelines section issued in 2010 by the National Science Foundation (NSF).

In addition to the information requested below, there were also pages of forms, legal descriptions and assurances. Note the order of items that are requested for the proposal document. The order in which they appear below is generally the exact order required by most funding guidelines.

The following elements are required in sequential order in the NSF's general set of guidelines:

- Cover Sheet
- Project Summary
- Table of Contents
- Project Description—Objectives, Work Goals, Methods
- Results from Prior NSF Support
- Bibliographical Sketches
- Budgetary Items
- Current and Pending Support
- Facilities, Equipment
- Special Information
- Appendices

Within each of the major categories are sets of sub-categories. Each one must be addressed or you lose points. As proposals are reviewed by the funding group points are awarded by category. Often these are listed in the specific guidelines.

One word of caution is needed when applying to the NSF. The NSF requires a written merit statement by the proposer and the two criteria are listed below.

Criterion 1: What is the intellectual merit of the proposed activity?

How important is the proposed activity to advancing knowledge and understanding within its own field or across different fields? How well qualified is the proposer (individual or team) to conduct the project? (If appropriate, the reviewer will comment on the quality of prior work.) To what extent does the proposed activity suggest and explore creative and original concepts? How well conceived and organized is the proposed activity? Is there sufficient access to resources?

Criterion 2: What are the broader impacts of the proposed activity?

How well does the activity advance discovery and understanding while promoting teaching, training and learning? How well does the proposed activity broaden the participation of underrepresented groups (e.g., gender, ethnicity, disability, geographic, etc.)? To what extent will it enhance the infrastructure for research and education, such as facilities, instrumentation, networks and partnerships? Will the results be disseminated broadly to enhance scientific and technological understanding? What may be the benefits of the proposed activity to society?

The Directorate for Education and Human Resources of the NSF publishes a must-print-and-review 23-page booklet, "A Guide for Proposal Writing." Access this handy tool electronically at: www.nsf.gov.pub:2004/nsf0416/nsf0416.pdf. This guide has several helpful hints on preparing a successful proposal, specific to their process.

You absolutely must have the guidelines from any federal agency if you want to be successful. And what of the private sector?

Foundation Guidelines

In Chapter 2, we discussed some of the elements needed to contact foundations. To elaborate on those early themes, we have carefully selected the basic guidelines of a few American foundations. This is a fair representation of what the other thousands require in the way of an application.

A family very concerned with the environment founded the Weyerhaeuser Family Foundation, Inc. The Foundation report lists five program priorities for which they will fund projects: (1) Art and Humanities, (2) Education, (3) Environment, (4) Health and (5) International Affairs.

Applicants first complete a Letter of Intent that asks for basic information about the requesting group. The basics include contact information, your organization's finances and for which of the five priorities areas you are applying. The Letter of Intent is electronically sent. Currently they provide a 2 inch x 6 inch box in which you summarize your project. If you pass the Letter of Intent phase, you will be invited to submit a full proposal.

The W. K. Kellogg Foundation (made famous by corn flakes) lists six priority funding areas: Educated Kids, Health, Kids Secure Families, Civic Engagement, Racial Equality and International projects. The foundation has current assets over $529 million. How do you get your share?

As with most foundations, Kellogg has an on-line application format. Over 50 separate items are listed with a brief description of what must be included in that section. Of course, in several areas there are a maximum number of characters that may be typed electronically.

There are no deadlines and the Foundation personnel attempt to respond to each proposal within 45 days. For detailed information, go to: http://wrm.wkkf. org/uWebRequestManager/UI/Application.aspx.

We previously mentioned the John D. and Catherine T. MacArthur Foundation having assets in excess of $5.1 billion (not bad for a gentleman selling insurance). The guidelines list eight initiatives under which awards are made. The literature also states that they do not even accept applications for selected areas as noted in their guidelines. However, brochures with applications are also available for ten different programs. But what does MacArthur suggest? This foundation simply wants an initial letter of inquiry that does not exceed two or three pages. What do you include?

First, you include a cover sheet providing basic contact information about your organization. This is followed by the abstract of your project, which includes:

- Purpose
- Problem or issue and its significance to MacArthur's program or strategy.
- How the project work addresses the issue
- Qualification of your organization to do the work
- Relevance to MacArthur's initiatives
- Geographic area of project
- Dissemination plan
- Budget and estimated total request

Information may be obtained from John D. and Catherine T. MacArthur Foundation, 140 South Dearborn Street, Chicago, Illinois 60603-5285, or by contacting 4answers@macfound.org.

Using almost an identical format is the Carnegie Corporation of New York. In 1900, when Andrew Carnegie sold his steel empire to J. P. Morgan, he had a $400 million bank account. He believed it was a "moral obligation" to share one's fortunes once all basic needs had been cared for. As such, the Foundation now has total assets of $3 billion.

However, the Carnegie Guidelines do caution that many of their awards are for renewals. (Recall in Chapter 2 our note about asking program officers these questions.) Carnegie has no deadlines and typically responds in four to six weeks. They provide an online Letter of Inquiry format, obtainable at: http://Carnegie.org/grants/grantseekers/submitting-a-letter-of-inquiry.

No need to belabor the point. There are guidelines, get them, follow them carefully, and, for most, they will follow the generic model being illustrated in this book. (Who said that experience doesn't count?) Now let's focus on the problems and objectives portion of your proposal.

OBJECTIVES

In Chapter 1, we provided several examples of problem statements. Chapter 3 illustrated how needs statements are generated. It is essential to have these statements carefully crafted and developed. Naturally, you also introduce your proposal with a strong lead-in statement that sets the tone for what follows.

Depending on the guidelines, you will need a vision statement, amply covered in Chapter 1, or a statement of goals. Each of these items is a distinct element of a proposal. What are goals? Let us first answer in the negative: *They are not specific actions or objectives.* A goal is a broad framework. Goals are abstractions that inspire and guide actions. Goals are seldom attained, whereas objectives are. One broad goal for the schools is "to foster critical thinking." And as Lieberman (1956) wrote, "Be careful not to criticize anything important." That goal requires issues to be studied and values to be discussed openly. Will it be achieved?

But, for a grant proposal, if the goal is to provide students with the best that new technologies can offer, there is a requirement of specific objectives. We are not degrading goals at all. The point being made is that goals are general statements. The term "goal" is usually used interchangeably with "aims," "purpose," and "long-range outlook."

An objective describes exactly what will happen, be accomplished or take place. A goal is a very general statement and is then made very specific with a statement of action objectives. It is safe to say that every grant proposal requires a set of objectives. Further, the objectives must be perfectly aligned with the problem or need that has been established. Let us provide some examples.

To be certain that the objective statement is made clearly, we suggest the following item or lead: *The objectives of this proposal are to: . . .* In that manner, you are forced to provide a complete thought. Below we list examples of objective statements that may be useful as you model your own.

These objectives were listed in a small grant proposal that aimed to address the need to educate teachers on the use of portfolio assessment:

1. To implement an across-the-curriculum portfolio model in grades K-5.
2. To provide working knowledge to the staff about portfolio assessment models so they may select appropriate ones to meet our specific needs.
3. To focus the staff on student strengths and growth through portfolio assessments.
4. To provide a model for long-term assessment of student learning.

A study of occupational aspiration of women had two objectives.

1. This study will compare the differential effects of attending college upon the educational and occupational aspirations of men and women.

2. The second objective is to test levels of aspiration via two theoretical structures: "relative deprivation" and "environmental press."

The next example includes a goal statement followed by four specific objectives.

Goal. The proposal has two goals. The first is to provide a pre-service model that can be easily disseminated, adapted and implemented in not only land-grant universities, but in all universities having a similar administrative organization.

The second is to redress the collectively identified science deficiencies in teacher preparation existing nationally as well as on our own campus.

Objectives. The objectives of this proposal are to:

1. Design a physical science course for elementary majors with the intent of constructing a national model.
2. Integrate scientific epistemology and relevant science history within the science context.
3. Design appropriate laboratory activities.
4. Integrate modern media, e.g., the Web and microcomputers into the program.

The next two examples show that you need not follow one formula or lead-in to specify proposal objectives in an effective way:

Objectives of the Clinical Trial: It is hypothesized that estrogen replacement therapy (ERT) will reduce the risk of coronary heart disease [CHD] and of osteoporosis-related fractures. Because progestin and estrogen replacement therapies (PERT) are commonly used together in order to diminish the risk of endometrial cancer, a PERT arm will be included to assess whether the hypothesized beneficial effects on preventing coronary disease and fractures will be retained. The incidence of endometrial cancer and breast cancer will be monitored during and after the trial. The estimated sample size requirement for the outcome of this coronary heart disease is 25,000. This sample size would give power of 94 percent for detecting a 30 percent reduction in CHD incidence over nine (9) years.

Dietary modification in the form of a low-fat eating pattern is hypothesized to reduce the risk of breast cancer, colorectal cancer and coronary heart disease. The estimated sample size requirement for each of the outcomes of breast cancer and colorectal cancer is 48,000. The sample size gives a power of 81 percent for detecting a 15 percent reduction in breast cancer, and 94 percent power for detecting a 21 percent reduction in colorectal cancer incidence over nine (9) years.

49

This example shows a more diverse way of incorporating the aim, rationale and objectives. But do notice each statement begins with an action verb.

The primary aim of this research is to interface engineering technology with the field of cytapheresis research by investigating and developing an online approach to blood separator optimization. The method will take advantage of fundamental settling characteristics of cellular particles by adjusting cell concentrations with separated fraction recycle. Additional benefits of this effort will be that the optimizations will be accomplished without cell sedimenting agents and that cellular species in separated fractions will be determined online. To accomplish these tasks, the following specific objectives will be pursued.

1. Interface an online computer system to a cell counting system, an automated sampling system and an existing cell centrifuge. This will allow current information about the centrifuge to be collected and analyzed with the computer, as well as allowing the computer to control and optimize the operation of the centrifuge.

2. Combine the separation of blood at reduced HCT with recycle techniques to extend initial examinations of the basic sedimentation character of cellular species and clarify optimum operating modes of the centrifuge.

3. Investigate and develop an online optimization technique for the cell centrifuge which will predict the degree of separation as a function of operating parameters and change the operating parameters so that the maximum separation efficiency is obtained at all times.

4. Develop a method, using a Coulter counter interfaced with the laboratory computer, to estimate the total number of cells collected during a procedure.

5. Perform experiments to implement, test and verify the proposed online optimization technique.

Before closing, one more approach to writing objectives needs to be illustrated. Some guidelines will request a measurable objective or outcome. Assume that the goal of the project is to prepare bilingual tutors, and you're being asked to provide a measurable objective. It might read as:

After completion of the four-week ESL training program, 90 percent of the 20 trainees will be employed in the area's public schools as teacher-aides or student tutors.

These types of objectives are extremely specific. Use them only if requested, because you may not control the conditions necessary for success.

Common Errors in Writing Objectives

Please go back to the beginning of this section where models of objectives are illustrated, and count the objectives. Did you realize that these proposals included a maximum of only a handful of objectives? Keep the number of objectives to a manageable size. We have been on evaluation panels where proposals listed ten needs, nine outcomes and 16 objectives. This was not funded, because the writing was confusing and it was not clear what was actually going to be done by the grant applicant. Another proposal was rejected for having three broad goals and four value assumptions. These seven statements detracted from the needs.

However, it is not uncommon in big proposals or those that are multi-year to have several objectives. How do you reconcile this situation? You subdivide the objectives in subgroups, and for each subgroup, you state an overarching goal. For example: Subgroup One is to identify elements in the DNA that lead to dyslexia. The objectives are: [here the four would be listed].

Subgroup Two is to test these elements in groups of individuals identified as being dyslexic. Objectives of Subgroup Two: [here would be listed four or five objectives]. In this manner, you not only show good organization, you also illustrate that complex projects can be made more manageable.

Another common error in stating objectives is to combine both the objective and the means by which it will be attained. These complex statements are usually very lengthy and only confuse the panel members as they read them.

A third common error is to restate the needs or problem as an objective. Remember, the need is a condition; the problem is a statement being proposed for solution.

Finally, some objectives are not objectives at all. Proposal writers begin discussing some feature of the project and tend never to write any specific or achievable objective.

Once the objectives have been written, you have the vital elements of the blueprint and can begin to add the details on how you will complete each one.

Depending on the guidelines, a review of research often follows the objectives. We cover that section next.

CONDUCTING A LITERATURE SEARCH FOR GRANT PROPOSALS

A literature search is the process of examining sources of information on a given subject that exist in several places and in various forms for the purpose of obtaining important background information for use in providing the rationale for a proposal or research design. Such information may be obtained from published articles, funded proposals and equipment catalogs or through personal communications. As implied, all references need not be of a printed nature, but could be telephone conversations or interviews, for example. However, they do need to be verifiable, hence careful notes should be made of non-print sources. The "literature" search is usually done after the need for a proposed action has been explored. Do seek advice from colleagues or others engaged in related activities, to determine feasibility and interest.

What Are the Purposes of a Literature Search?

Basically, there are four main purposes. The first is to acquaint the reader with (a) existing studies relative to what is being proposed, (b) who has done similar work, (c) when and where the latest studies were completed and (d) what approaches involving methodology, instrumentation and statistical analyses were followed.

The second purpose is to establish a possible need for the proposed project and the likelihood for obtaining meaningful, relevant and significant results. You show that your idea works, is sound and is also different, and will add to the body of knowledge.

The third purpose is to provide a conceptual framework from which a rationale for the proposed project may be developed.

What Are Some of the More Important Sources?

General references such as the *Review of Educational Research* or *Psychological Bulletin* contain summaries of previous work related to a given problem situation or research problem. Do seek the most prestigious journals in your discipline. And do seek research, not opinions. Specific books, monographs, bulletins, reports and research articles—preferably those written very recently—are all useful.

Unpublished materials can be excellent sources, e.g., dissertations or papers presented at recent professional meetings not yet in published form, but available through such sources as ERIC (Education Resources Information Center). Often the most recent studies will be refereed papers given at professional meetings.

Government publications, previously funded proposals, and reports from funding agencies about similar projects are great sources. Using published studies from a funding agency will impress the program officer that you know their material.

A preliminary review of the subject should be made so that you understand the terminology, background and limitations of published studies. To help find more sources, refer to the citations in the most important studies. Check these sources for further leads. This process should be continued until there is an overlap among cited articles. This technique is called a "fan search," since each paper contains a bibliography that spreads out like a fan.

As you conduct the literature search, stay focused. Temping as it may be, do not go off on tangents. Your review has to have a tight focus that supports your objectives and plan of operation.

Use primary sources for your key references. Keep in mind that you will be limited as to how extensive your proposal may be. Currently, the average is about 12 to 15 pages, single-spaced. A review of literature should be about one or, at maximum, two pages of the total 15.

NB: The National Institutes of Health (NIH) has eliminated the review of literature as a separate section, expecting instead to see the relevant citations in support of the proposal inserted as integral components of the proposal.

Presenting the Findings

Once you have all the literature organized, you'll need to summarize the key points. Select and arrange the literature in a manner that is parallel with your own format. For example, if you state questions, hypotheses or specific aims in your problem statements, then structure the review in the same order. This consistent organization aids reviewers and, if they do not have to reread previous sections, you'll receive a positive ranking by the evaluation panel members. Be sure to highlight the critical information pieces. Please do not list an entire line with citations for some self-evident point. In this regard, "laundry lists" of citations detract from points being made. You don't need to cite extensive passages unless the original writer stated it so profoundly the key idea will be missed if you paraphrase.

A Literature Search

The nature of a proposal will determine whether or not a literature search will be needed and how extensive it should be. For a basic research proposal, for example, a rigorous and exhaustive literature search may be required. When preparing a proposal for the purchase of a single piece of instructional scientific equipment, it may be sufficient to indicate that the most recent equipment catalog was used to obtain the cost and description of the equipment requested.

Proposals vary in their need to contain evidence of a literature search. When proposing the purchase and use of computer equipment for instructional purposes, a clear rationale should be given regarding how the decision to purchase the particular piece of equipment was reached. Such a decision should be based upon an examination of the successful use of such equipment under similar circumstances at other institutions. Similarly, the use of new educational techniques and technologies, such as Computer-Assisted Instruction (CAI) or Personalized System of Instruction (PSI), should be well documented with evidence that they are appropriate for the local setting.

In the proposal printed in Appendix A, you can observe one model of a literature review that is focused on the project's aim.

A SUMMARY AS A WORKING BLUEPRINT

One helpful device that we recommend in preparing grant proposals is the project summary or abstract. This short document briefly lists the need, objectives, general statement of procedures and the evaluation. This piece helps the writing team members and ensures that everyone knows what is being planned. Of course, this statement will be rewritten two, three or four times, for it must accurately reflect the whole project.

Keep in mind that often the summary will be the very first page read by the reviewers. You want it to read perfectly. Refine it. Rewrite it. Edit it. Make certain it says what you want to say in precisely the right words. Word selection is critical. A proposal faces its most important evaluation when the reviewer reads that initial statement.

In keeping with the idea that you should be exposed to several different forms, we will illustrate three in the subsequent models and close with two more checklists for your use.

MODEL 4.1: Plant Research

The overall objectives of this research are to fully understand the chemical nature of the systemic response of plants to pest attacks or wounding that result in the regulation of expression of proteinase inhibitor genes. More specifically, research is planned to (1) identify, isolate and characterize the chemical signal(s) that is (are) released and transported throughout tomato plants in response to wounding; (2) determine the mechanism(s) by which the systemic wound signals are released; (3) determine the mechanism(s) of signal reception in target cells and determine the nature of the intracellular mechanism results in the regulation of expression of proteinase inhibitor genes.

MODEL 4.2: State Budgeting for Higher Education Practice and Theory

Objectives

State budget formulation is an important process that is seriously lacking documentation. State budgeting agencies are under heavy pressure to improve budget practice in relation to higher education, despite uncertainties surrounding the effectiveness of existing budgeting techniques and policy formulation. The increasing competition for state revenue, the lack of increases in productivity, the redistribution of enrollments among institutions, the demands for cost and productivity information and the incongruity between educational expectations and available resources — all place strains on the budgeting process. Information regarding this process is scattered and not readily available. Therefore, the major objective of this study is to provide information and guidelines to improve state budget formulations for post-secondary educations. A second objective is to test certain theoretical concepts in inter-organizational cooperation, Program Planning and Budgeting Systems, Management by Objectives and others in order to develop a theory about resource allocation processes.

Methods and Procedures

The study will conduct a field investigation in 18 states supplemented by a questionnaire survey of all 50 states. Selected propositions of organizational theory will be tested with data collected in the field investigation. The study is a three-year effort that will provide state-level policymakers with a broad perspective of budget formulation across all of its elements. The project will provide the context for later, more informed assessments of the separate elements of budget formulation.

Significance

The information and guidelines developed from this study will play an important role in building a state system for the delivery of career education. This system is to be one of the priorities for career education during the next few years. It will include post-secondary education as one of its elements, and a thorough knowledge of state budgeting policies and practices for higher education is a necessary component of the total system. The estimated cost is $341,620.

MODEL 4.3: A Statewide System to Promote the Implementation of New Programs in Science, Mathematics and Social Studies

Project Director:

Donald C. Orlich

Estimated Cost:

$25,000 each year

The Problem:

There is a need to provide a prototype system for a statewide mechanism to diffuse curricular innovations in elementary and middle school science, mathematics and social sciences. This need would be reduced by coordinating the plans, activities and structures of four already-existing agencies: National Science Foundation, Washington State University (WSU), Washington Office of the State Superintendent of Public Instruction and Washington Educational Service Districts (ESDs), which encompass the state's 299 operating school districts.

Objectives:

The specific objectives of this project are to:

1. Provide intensive preparation during the summer to curriculum specialists selected by the Washington ESDs to create resource personnel for "Science — A Process Approach" (SAPA), "Science Curriculum Improvement Study" (SCIS) and "Elementary School Science" (ESS). Six other programs will be selected for the subsequent summers.
2. Provide each resource person with sets of diffusion strategies and paradigms for presenting in-service orientation programs on the selected curricula in the respective ESDs.
3. Establish and evaluate a model for a statewide dissemination and diffusion network.

Procedures:

A series of three intensive summer workshops will be conducted on campus at WSU. Participants in these resource personnel workshops will be curriculum specialists designated by the ESDs. The resource persons will be prepared to understand the rationale, structure and materials of each program and will return to the respective ESDs to conduct a series of awareness-information workshops on the programs. An evaluation of the system will be concurrently conducted through use of data-collecting instruments to determine the number of awareness workshops conducted and the number of adoptions of "new" programs.

Significance of Project:

This system could be a prototype model for other states. The plan is conceptually similar to the change-agent model, which has been so effective in the nation's agricultural sector.

CHECKLIST: Introduction/Problem/Objectives

Circle the letter to the left that best describes your evaluation of that element. A written statement to help the writer improve should follow anything less than the highest rating.

Introduction

1. The initial statements provide:
    a. Very smooth transition for the reader
    b. An implied transition
    c. Some disconnectedness
    d. Some confusion

2. The introductory paragraph:

    a. Provides a general idea to the reader

    b. Leads the reader to the problem

    c. Seems choppy

    d. Seems to be abrupt

3. The introduction **as written**:

    a. Is well developed and crafted

    b. Needs some editing

    c. Needs major rewriting

    d. Detracts from the problem

Problem or Need

1. Significance of the problem **as written**:

    a. Rather significant

    b. Moderately significant

    c. Rather insignificant

    d. Very insignificant

2. Clarity of statement of the problem:

    a. Very clear

    b. Rather clear

    c. Somewhat ambiguous

    d. Rather obscure

3. Documentation is provided or cited to substantiate the problem or need:

    a. Citations or data provided

    b. Some data given

    c. Implied, but not cited

    d. No documentation

4. The problem section is stated:

    a. Explicitly

    b. Somewhat explicitly, but needs focus

    c. Somewhat inexplicitly

    d. Very inexplicitly

Objectives

1. Relationship of the objectives to the stated problem:

    a. Well integrated

    b. Moderately integrated

    c. Incomplete

    d. Reflects lack of precision

2. Extent to which objectives are clearly or succinctly stated:
    a. Very clear
    b. Rather clear, but some revisions needed
    c. Too wordy
    d. Obscure
3. The number of objectives seem to be:
    a. Adequate
    b. In need of some recombining
    c. Somewhat redundant
    d. Excessive
4. My overall rating of the objectives section is:
    a. Excellent
    b. Good
    c. Adequate, but needs polish
    d. Inadequate

CHECKLIST: Evaluation Checklist for Project Abstracts or Summaries

The numerical rating codes to the right should be interpreted to mean:

NA Not Applicable to Project
1   Very Inadequately Stated
2   Inadequately Stated
3   Adequately Stated
4   Very Adequately Stated

Elements	Ratings			
1. The introduction clearly "sets the stage."		1	2	3	4
2. Problem or need is clearly stated.		1	2	3	4
3. The problem or need is significant within the context of this abstract.		1	2	3	4
4. Objectives are clearly stated.		1	2	3	4
5. Hypotheses are clearly stated.	NA	1	2	3	4
6. Relationship of the problem or need to previous research is clearly stated.	NA	1	2	3	4
7. Significance of projected results stated.	NA	1	2	3	4
8. Research design is appropriate to problem solution.	NA	1	2	3	4

9. Project procedures are appropriate to problem
   solution.   NA 1   2   3   4

10. Methods are identified to analyze data.   NA 1   2   3   4

11. Evaluation section focuses on objectives.   NA 1   2   3   4

12. Abstract is clearly written.   1   2   3   4

13. Abstract is logically organized.   1   2   3   4

14. Abstract is written in an unbiased manner.   1   2   3   4

15. Overall ranking of total abstract.   1   2   3   4

Chapter 5

Procedures, Management and Evaluation

CHAPTER SUMMARY

- The Procedures Section
- Timelines
- Staffing
- Evaluation Considerations
- Procedures Checklist

The development of the proposal follows a "logic ladder." The needs or problem statement leads to the objectives. The objectives then lead to the procedures. It is in this section of the proposal where each objective is fully amplified. Depending on your guidelines, the section is labeled "methodology," "work plan," "project activities" or "scope of operation." You label it whatever your guidelines request. For the purposes of this chapter, we'll refer to the section as "procedures."

THE PROCEDURES SECTION

What are procedures? Procedures are the explanations of how you will accomplish each objective. You restate each objective and in detail give answers to the following:

- Who will be involved?
- What precisely will take place?
- When will the activities take place?
- Where will the activities take place?
- Why is this approach being used?

In some larger proposals, the review of literature is interwoven with the specific procedures. For example, if this were a chemistry equipment grant proposal, you would then provide a short review showing how the equipment would add to research knowledge.

In addition, you would address the key functions:

- Planning that takes place.
- Organizing the human and other resources.
- Staffing the project.
- Directing activities.
- Coordinating the project elements.
- Budgeting responsibility.

You may have recognized POSDCORB approach, the functional approach to management made famous in 1937 by Lyndall F. Gulick and Luther L. Urwick. We recommend using POSDCORB when completing the procedure section because it requires you to account for all the functions of successful project management. Again, these are the details that must be addressed in the procedures section. Refer to the model proposal illustrated in Appendix A.

TIMELINES

In many guidelines, you are asked to prepare a PERT Chart (Program Evaluation Review Technique) or a Gantt Chart. These are timelines illustrating who is responsible for what and when specific events are scheduled.

To prepare any timeline model, you brainstorm with the writing team to identify the key tasks. These ideas are sorted and displayed in a logical and chronological order. Examine Models 5.1, 5.2 and 5.3 for partially completed timeline formats.

We have deliberately not illustrated a PERT Chart due to space and art limitations. But for many PERT Models, refer to Desmond L. Cook's excellent work (1978) cited in the References section. Many PERT Chart models can be accessed electronically at: www.google.com/#hI=entsource=hp&q=pert+charts+examples&aq=1&aqi=g1.

STAFFING

It is imperative that you list all the persons who will participate in the project, assuming it will be funded. This is important since in the budget you will be paying for their specific services. If you do not list the people in the narrative portion of the proposal, then you cannot provide a budgeted item. We recommend you have

MODEL 5.1: A Partially Completed Activity and Responsibility Chart

Activity	Responsibility	Product	Time
1. Review Purpose and Goals	Advisory Group	Assignment of Tasks	
2. Literature Search	Project Assistants	Summary of Relevant Articles	
3. Devise Survey Instrument	Project Director and Assistants	Copies for Pre-test	
4. Evaluate Instrument	Advisory Group	Suggested Revisions	
5. Distribute Instrument	Project Assistants	Complete Distribution	
6. Process and Analyze Data	Project Director and Assistants	Tallied Results	
7. Write Final Report	Project Director and Assistants	Draft for Review	
8. Seminar on Results	Project Director	Further Dissemination	

all people committed before the proposal is finalized. Some agencies require an actual letter of commitment from personnel listed in the proposal. So, plan well in advance.

Observe the manner in which the personnel are listed in the Model Proposal in Appendix A. The responsibilities of each person are listed. Any program officer or review panel member can see that much planning has gone into the proposal and that key responsibilities and functions are identified in advance. That is the essence of effective planning.

You'll also need to include a vita or resume for key personnel, i.e., project director, assistant director and others involved in the project. Be sure to read the guidelines that you are following, to ensure you're following the proper format. In general, the vitae should be uniformly organized. In many cases, some project leaders will not have a current vita. If that is so, then use Model 5.4 as a worksheet by which to standardize the display of vitae. "Quality of Personnel" is often a major evaluative criterion by which your proposal will be judged. Be certain that everyone's strengths are highlighted as they apply to the project.

Model 5.4 should be prepared on at least three or four pages, allowing ample space under each main entry for insertions. These worksheets are collected, edited and prepared in a uniform format for all key players. Check the guidelines that you are following, as many limit the number of pages per vitae.

MODEL 5.2: A Partial Timeline for Project Activities

Week	1	3	5	7	9	11	13	15	17	19	21	23	25	27	29	31
	2	4	6	8	10	12	14	16	18	20	22	24	26	28	30	32

TASK #1   __7__   __8__   __9__   __10__
START

    __2__

     __3__

      __4__

       __5__   6

1. Start-up September 15
2. Review of Principles
3. Establishment of Formats and Designs
4. Refinement of Steps 2 and 3
5. Selection of Pilot Test Personnel
6. Progress Reported to Agency
7. Preparation of Preliminary Draft for Pilot Testing
8. Administration of Instrument
9. Analysis of Results
10. Preparation and Submission of Final Report

If you are alone on the project, then you are "chief cook and bottle washer." But, you need a vita and you must describe what you will do. Again, check the guidelines for the scope of all vitae.

EVALUATION CONSIDERATIONS

Many agencies require the grant application to illustrate its efficacy or its potential to advance knowledge in a specific discipline, i.e., some internal evaluation. All evaluation is subjective. Now, we've carefully chosen that predicate. We did not write "arbitrary," "capricious," "biased" or "objective." Subjective means that *you* determine what should be evaluated, how and to what magnitude of fidelity. But one tip will save you much grief. Employ the ladder logic again. The objectives should drive the evaluation; therefore, focus the evaluation on the degree of attainment of the objectives.

63

MODEL 5.3: Partially Complete Gantt Chart

Descriptors	Year One						Year Two					
	2	4	6	8	10	12	2	4	6	8	10	12
1. Review of Practices—Project Paper												
Review Literature		—										
Write Paper			—									
Produce				—								
Distribute				—								
Deliver to NSF												
2. Teaching Documents Set #1												
Collect Materials			—									
Review Materials	—	—	—	—	—	—						
Document Exemplary School Practices												
	—	—	—	—	—	—						
Describe Products (1st Version)			—									
Revise			—									
Evaluate Document Usefulness				—								
Produce Documents					—							
Distribute to Test Sites							—					
Deliver Set to NSF												

For example, if you have an objective to provide in-service training, then your evaluation model should focus on the participants' opinion of the training and perhaps how much the participants learned as a consequence of the project and the impact it has had on practice.

If the project were to design and implement some specific physical science materials, then the evaluation would follow that line. Keep the evaluation objective; yes, but also keep it simple. If you have a multi-year, big proposal, then do you need a complex evaluation model? For the most part, you don't.

In addition to evaluating the objectives, it is also recommended that you list a set of questions that will guide the evaluation process. For example, "Do teachers change their instructional methods as a consequence of attending inquiry-oriented workshops?" "How effective are short-term workshops to implement new

MODEL 5.4: Vita Worksheet

PRELIMINARIES

Full Name	Mailing Address
Title	Telephone
Organization	Fax
	E-mail

HIGHER EDUCATION

Degree, University, City, Major, Date

NB: Use separate entries for B.A., M.A., Ph.D.

ADDITIONAL EDUCATIONAL EXPERIENCES

Specify post B.A., M.A. or Ph.D. work, special institutes, seminars and workshops of at least six hours' duration. If leaders are known, list them also and be sure to list location. If you attended an invited seminar, be certain to note that.

PROFESSIONAL EXPERIENCES

List your occupational records.

Veterans—list service dates.

List date, position, rank or title (most recent on top to less recent).

PROFESSIONAL AWARDS

List biographies, recognition from professional groups, awards and prizes. Here is a section in which modesty must be placed aside. All honors that have been received should be listed.

LEADERSHIP POSITIONS AND COMMITTEES

List leadership positions held in all professional organizations, especially note service on various committees, e.g., curriculum, research, awards committees, scholarship committees, program, evaluation.

PROFESSIONAL ORGANIZATONS

Provide listing of current memberships in all professionally related organizations. If you are a "life member," so note.

PROFESSIONAL ACTIVITIES AND SERVICES

List consultancies, evaluation teams, review panels, addresses delivered, service that you rendered.

PROFESSIONAL PUBLICATIONS

Use a standard bibliographic format and list major or all published works.

GRANTS, PROPOSALS, REPORTS

List only funded grant proposals; give title of grant, funding agency, date and amount. Also list proposals pending and reports that you authored or co-authored. The reports need not be published.

program?" These questions would then be answered by designing appropriate evaluation techniques. Below are a few models and techniques that have appeared in published literature on the topic. Depending on the type of project that you want funded, your evaluation model should be congruent with it.

Formative and Summative Evaluation

Let us begin with a model initially described by M. C. Scriven (1967) and which is most applicable in training or curriculum implementation projects.

Formative evaluation is designed to provide feedback in a rather immediate sense. Formative strategies are specifically designed to monitor aspects of any group to determine where problems may be emerging. By using formative evaluation, problems will be quickly identified and rectified. For example, if some methodology were being used which caused the participants to do poorly, it would be through frequent use of formative evaluation that troubleshooting would take place. By continuously checking the "small steps," project directors might identify potentially detrimental learning or even instructional problems. Formative evaluation techniques should be initiated so that instructors can observe many different perspectives of the program while it is actually in operation. This is imperative for carefully sequenced topics or where critical prerequisite skills are being learned. Model 5.5 illustrates one feedback form that co-author Orlich used in conducting NSF-funded workshops for several years, where teachers are brought in for six weeks of research with research engineers.

Only a few selected items need to be checked during any one formative evaluation. These would all be based on the stated project objectives. You do not need a lengthy listing of items. The important point is that the feedback is collected while there is adequate time to make adjustments in the project's operations.

The rationale for formative evaluation is to provide data on which to make correctives—immediately, if not sooner! When participants and program staff members alike realize that they are being constantly monitored and helped, they tend to become more responsible and become more productive. The instructional climate and total environment become positive and supportive.

That is precisely the kind of learning climate to which one always ought to subscribe when teaching. Conversely, projects have "gone on the rocks" because the project director was not evaluating project activities over short periods of time, but waited until the very end of the project to accomplish a one-shot final evaluation only to find it had failed.

Formative evaluation requires that the project director carefully observe a selected set of *experiences* for all participants. For example, with science programs, some form of laboratory activity is used to build a cluster of generic skills for future use. A person using formative evaluation would monitor the skills and when

MODEL 5.5: Project Feedback

Directions: Place an "X" on each line above the category which best describes your reactions.

1. How has the project progressed to date?

   Moving Very Slowly   Could Move Faster   Moving Along Nicely

2. How is your participation in this project?

   Not With It At All   Could Be More Involved   Really With It

3. Is the organization and conduct of the project meeting your expectations?

   Not At All   Meeting Some and   Meeting All and
   Not Meeting Others   Then Some

4. How adequately will you be able to make an easy adjustment of translating the content from this project to your own classes?

   Very Inadequately   Inadequately   Adequately   Very Adequately

5. Comments or Suggestions

   _____

   _____

   _____

a participant did poorly, a new set of experiences would be provided. To correct any noted learning deficiency, one does not wait to take the "final exam." Correctives are an integral part of the formative evaluation plan.

One simple method by which to record formative data is to tabulate the absolute numbers or percentages of both individual and group activities. A project director could compare group data on a graph so that the directions of the groups could be visually displayed for instant analysis.

The essential characteristic of formative evaluation is that "hard data" are being collected so that they may add a more "objective" evaluation of what is usually considered as "soft data" or the subjective elements of evaluation. But, more importantly, correctives are built into the scheme, so that feedback is used when it is needed most—not stored for the future.

The evaluation which is conducted as the final or concluding task is called the *summative evaluation*. It should be noted that summative evaluation might be the final formative evaluation of a project. Summative evaluations may take several forms, just so that they are consistent with the prescribed objectives of the program. Again, summative data could be tabulated into absolute responses and then as a percentage for each item. Comparisons between students could also be made on summative data (but not usually on the formative measures).

Summative test data could then be arranged in a profile to illustrate the sum of evaluation activities. Formative data provide feedback, while the summative scores lead to "judgments" about the quality of performances.

Most projects fail because evaluation is a one-shot post-evaluation. Such an evaluation strategy can never aid a project director. The information comes when the project is over! Of course, it may be argued that formative and summative techniques will cause the direction of the project to change. Why, yes, we agree; and we would submit that, if properly used, the objectives of the project might be altered. Success is the underlying tenet of this evaluation technique. If a program, course or project needs to be modified because of unrealistic expectations (objectives), then why not alter it? One word of caution: If you alter a stated objective, be sure to contact your funding agency's program officer to receive approval.

Perhaps the most compelling reason in support of the formative and summative model is that there are really no "surprises" at the end of the project. With early feedback systems being built into the system, all elements converge toward success. Model 5.6 illustrates one successfully used model.

Achievement Tests

Achievement tests are constructed to assess a participant's terminal behavior or the expected behavior or attainment after completion of a project. Achievement tests are developed to assess the degree or quality to which the desired behavior or performance takes place. Such test scores tend to show a level of current skill development.

Achievement scores provide two types of information: (1) the individual's level of skill or knowledge relative to an established level of quality control, and (2) the relative ordering (rank) of the individual's score in relation to the rest of the class. Robert Glaser (1963) refers to the first type of information as criterion-referenced measures and states that these measures depend upon an absolute standard of quality. This means that the participant either has or has not acquired the predetermined mastery level of the skill. The degree of skill attainment is usually stated in some descriptive term. The second type of information is usually referred to as norm referenced, since it compares a student with other students in a selected group.

Glaser refers to the student's level of achievement as occurring somewhere on a hypothetical continuum of knowledge or skill proficiency ranging from zero (e.g., the student cannot balance an oxidation-reduction equation) to mastery (the student can balance all oxidation-reduction equations). Generally, achievement tests are norm referenced.

However, for a few years, co-author Orlich and his colleagues had developed criterion-referenced measures in elementary science. All test items are

MODEL 5.6:   Summative Evaluation for Short-Term Workshops

Directions: Please circle the number to the right of each statement that best describes your evaluation of each item.

1 = Totally Inadequate
2 = Poor
3 = Somewhat Positive or Somewhat Negative
4 = Good
5 = Excellent

1. The specified goals of the project were:	1	2	3	4	5
2. The climate or atmosphere of the project was:	1	2	3	4	5
3. The overall design of the project was:	1	2	3	4	5
4. The start-up, introductory activities were:	1	2	3	4	5
5. The staff, in terms of concern and awareness of the participants, was:	1	2	3	4	5
6. The manner in which the participants could influence the direction of the project was:	1	2	3	4	5
7. The use of the staff resources during the project was:	1	2	3	4	5
8. The articulation of content to science classes during the project was:	1	2	3	4	5
9. The "experiential" or "hands-on" activities used in the project were:	1	2	3	4	5
10. My overall rating of this "project" is:	1	2	3	4	5

11. Comments:

_____

_____

keyed only to the activities being used. They administered the same test pre- and post-compute means and standard deviations, and then computed an effect size to determine the learning gain for participants in the training sessions and for students as well.

The effect size is expressed as a decimal or mixed number. For example, an effect size of 1.0 can be interpreted as a gain of one standard deviation on a normal curve for the treatment group. An effect size of 2.0 is phenomenal and equates to a 48-percentile gain! At 0.30, an effect size becomes useful or important having a 12-percentile gain. Effect sizes less than 0.2 are usually not important. An effect size of 0.25 begins to show importance, or a 10-percentile gain.

To calculate the effect size, one subtracts the mean score of the pre-test from the mean score of the post-test and then divides the difference by the standard deviation of the pre-test. For example, on a post-test, assume that the group had a mean of 90, while the mean of the pre-test was 80 with a standard deviation of 8.0 points. The difference of the means, or 10, is divided by 8 for a 1.25 effect size (a 40-percentile gain). Stay with that treatment, it's a winner. By the way, many researchers do not report their test scores in such a manner, so one cannot compute an effect size. We wonder why?

For discussion about effect size, see G. V. Glass (1976, 1980); J. Cohen (1988); B. S. Bloom (1984); R. J. Marzano et al. (2001); and two monumental works that report scores of treatments and effect sizes, by H. J. Walberg (1991) and J. C. Hattie (2009).

Other Evaluation Techniques

Depending on the project objectives, there are several other techniques that may be employed to evaluate success.

The first is to observe pre- and post-behaviors of the participants. This is a powerful method, especially where new curricula or teaching methods are being stressed. Observational techniques are, however, labor-intensive, thus, expensive.

The second is to employ participant journals. This strategy approximates a case study or qualitative approach to evaluation.

The third technique is the judging of some project or achievement. Many individuals are funded to produce training tapes, print materials, computer software or some product. A panel could be used to evaluate these artifacts.

Single subject design (time series) is yet a fourth technique that could be employed as an evaluation model. We would suggest contacting the National Science Foundation to obtain a copy of their published monograph on project evaluation. The title of the free piece, address and URL are listed below.

J. F. Westat, editor, et al., *The 2002 User-Friendly Handbook for Project Evaluation*, 2002. Directorate for Education and Human Resources, National Science Foundation, Arlington, VA 22230. This handbook can be accessed at: www. nsf.gov/pubs/2002/nsf02057/nsf02057.pdf

D. L. Stufflebeam and A. J. Shinkfield (2007) identified several major evaluation models, their assumptions and uses. This handy reference will yield a wide array of techniques by which to evaluate your proposal.

Finally, there is the use of a "third-party contract," in which you place the evaluation out on bid. The main elements for such a subcontract are:

- Purpose or evaluation questions to be answered
- Services or products to be provided
- Qualifications of evaluators
- Scheduling specifications

- Evaluation plans
- Nature of reports
- Assurances
- Budget and payment schedule

A third-party subcontract is a good idea when you have a very large grant (in excess of $200,000) and one that is multi-year in duration. You have a greater probability of "objectivity" if someone other than you conducts the evaluation who is not associated with your organization. At least that is the rationale.

Since the procedures are key to any proposal's funding, we close with a checklist to judge your procedures section.

CHECKLIST: Procedures

Circle the number that describes the component being evaluated.

       1 = Very Inadequate
       2 = Inadequate
       3 = Neither Inadequate Nor Adequate
       4 = Adequate
       5 = Very Adequate

1. The introduction provides a clear and logical lead
   to the problem.   1 2 3 4 5

2. The problem/need is explicitly stated.   1 2 3 4 5

3. The objectives describe *what* will take place.   1 2 3 4 5

4. The procedures relate to the needs or problem.   1 2 3 4 5

5. The procedures relate to the objectives.   1 2 3 4 5

6. The procedures explicitly illustrate how each objective
   will be implemented.   1 2 3 4 5

7. The procedures show a *logical* sequencing.   1 2 3 4 5

8. The procedures, as prepared, show a definite
   sequence of activities.   1 2 3 4 5

9. The proposal provides reasons for the selection of
   the activities.   1 2 3 4 5

10. Other: (Specify)

_____

_____

Chapter 6

Calculating a Budget

CHAPTER SUMMARY

- Basic Principles
- Facilities and Administrative Costs (Indirect Costs)
- Other Budgeting Considerations
- Budget Checklist

The budget actually consists of two sections: The first is a tallying of figures, while the second is the budget justification. The latter requires a rationale for each figure shown on the budget summary sheet. These aspects will be developed below. There are at least twelve basic principles that guide preparation of the proposal budget. Let us present them now.

BASIC PRINCIPLES

Principle 1. Always follow the guidelines. While this may be redundant, self-evident or repetitive, it is critical. Carefully examine what costs are allowed, which costs must be matched, and what costs are not allowed. A simple examination of the guidelines will alleviate budget renegotiations or just plain rejection of your proposal.

Principle 2. Never ask for more than you need. Yes, we all may have heard how to "pad" a budget. But, quite frankly, padding is an ethically dubious technique. What is your best estimate for each category? Check each with your accounting office. And, above all, be absolutely honest about the numbers.

Principle 3. You get what you earn. Now what does that mean? It means that no matter what you think you are worth, you get exactly the same salary on "soft" money as you do on the "hard" money. NB:In grant circles "soft" money is that obtained by grants or contracts and has a deadline date, whereas "hard" money means that which is a regular appropriation, usually for the biennium. Salaries cannot be inflated just because somebody else is paying for them!

Principle 4. If it is not in the narrative, it won't get funded. Principle 4 is most important, especially for novice grant proposal writers. Often they assume that simply "plugging in" a few figures will suffice. No! You must have every activity described in the narrative. You must identify everyone in the proposal who will eventually be paid. Obviously, you may not have every name listed. But you must identify the job position and what will be done. Program officers will "red-line" any item appearing in the budget that is not documented or identified in the narrative.

Principle 5. Projections are all right. The "kids may be all right" and so are multi-year budget projections. For example, many fiscal agents use the Consumer Price Index figures to predict future salaries. Obviously you know the salary you made this year. But four years subsequently it should be higher. Establish some "projected percentage rates of increase" and keep them constant throughout the budget. Most universities have established these rates in their fiscal offices.

Principle 6. Don't forget the fringe benefits. If part or all of a salary or wages is being paid by the grant, then so is that proportion of the fringe benefits. Fringe benefits include FICA (social security), retirement plans and health insurance payments, among others. For state or private institutions, these are all carefully specified in a master agreement. However, some non-profit organizations need to have an adopted list of fringe benefits so that they do not lose money when a grant is awarded. Or worse yet, require that you pay out-of-pocket for them. It is all totally legitimate. Consider that for many senior IHE employees the total fringe benefit package exceeds 35 percent of a person's salary.

Principle 7. You get paid in proportion to the scheduled work. If you work on project activities for 25 percent of the academic year, then all that you can make from the grant is 25 percent of your salary and fringe benefits.

Principle 8. You only get 100 percent. No matter how you complain or show that you are working 60 hours per week, you only get paid for a 40-hour workweek and your grant-paid salary cannot exceed 100 percent of your actual "hard money" salary. You may not, in most cases, get paid overtime.

There is one exception. If the work being done is above or beyond your regular work assignments, then you may be paid "extra compensation." Those two magic words must be noted in the budget justification in advance. You cannot be paid overtime retroactively. For example, many professors will help conduct in-service training for K-12 teachers on Saturdays or after school. This is a case for justifying "extra compensation."

Principle 9. Designated services are reimbursed. Travel, supplies, materials, per diem, hotels, taxes, long distance costs, services, rentals are all legitimate budget items. But you must have any of these listed or written into the narrative. Yes, you can have your grant pay for you to attend the next Society of Research Administrators International (SRAI) convention. You simply add that point in your dissemination section.

Principle 10. Equipment is tough to come by. Sorry, unless that laptop computer is being used 100 percent of the time for training or is thoroughly justified in the narrative, you won't be allowed the purchase from most grants. There are "equipment grants." These are different from just trying to stock an empty storeroom. Contact the program officer about restraints and limits on equipment and any needed reporting requirements. Obviously, if your proposal is a research grant and you need a mass spectrometer, go ahead and request it. In chemistry a mass spec is necessary to do high-level analytical work. Without such an instrument, specific research would not be feasible. You justify this in your budget discussion.

Principle 11. What are the cost-sharing requirements? Some agencies require from 5 percent to 100 percent in matching funds. Double-check the guidelines. Can donated time be used as a match? Can newly purchased equipment be used? Must the match be cash? Find out before you prepare the proposal to save institutional embarrassment.

A caution is needed here. If time is used, be certain that your time effort equals 100 percent, including the matching effort. Overtime is usually not allowed when time is used as a budgetary match. And time cost-sharing efforts must be documented by written time certifications. Let's elaborate on this often-"taken-lightly" practice.

Cost-sharing should be kept to the minimum as required by the guidelines. Cost-sharing is a requirement by many agencies and some foundations wherein not all allowable costs are funded. This means that the institution must fund a portion of the total budget. If there is no requirement in the guidelines, institutional research officers probably will not allow you to propose cost-sharing or matching. Cost-sharing and -matching (other than in-kind) are real (monetary) contributions or burdens on the institution and should be used wisely. Further, all non-funded support, such as cost-sharing, -matching or in-kind support, creates a significant administrative burden on both the principal investigator and the central and unit administrators of the organization.

NB: If you are asked to submit a revised budget to the funding agency, then by all means go back and revise the "cost-sharing" aspects of the proposal. Your institution is committed to whatever cost-sharing has been described in the final and approved budget.

If you do not meet your cost-sharing commitment, the institution is in great jeopardy of losing the funding, and may risk possible further ramifications, such as institutional penalties or forfeiture of rights to propose future projects to some funding organizations. Cost-sharing is a serious commitment and should be used prudently.

Principle 12. There is a termination date. Every grant has a beginning date when you may legally draw against the grant and a terminal or closing date. If, for any reason, you find you need more time, but not more money, to finish the project, then request a "no cost extension" from your program officer. These requests must be made at least 60 days in advance of the termination date for most agencies. However, the NIH now requires a 90-day advance request.

Once the termination date has passed, and if you do not have an extension, then absolutely no additional funds may be charged against the project.

A dozen principles are enough for anyone. Check your guidelines and, if you have any budgetary question, call the program officer and your finance officer for local policies. Those folks know what you are going through and they'll be most happy to provide suggestions.

What about facilities and administrative costs (indirect costs)?

FACILITIES AND ADMINISTRATIVE COSTS (INDIRECT COSTS)

Facilities and Administration Costs (F&A) (indirect costs) are often called "overhead" or "administrative costs." These are budgeted allocations made to grant-recipient institutions by nearly all federal agencies, but only by a tiny number of foundations. Note how carefully that last point was stated "to grant-recipient institutions," not to the project director. The F&A costs *are added* to the direct costs being charged against a grant to conduct the actual project.

Examine the budget of the model grant proposal in Appendix A. You will observe the direct costs of salaries and wages, fringe benefits, supplies, travel, per diem, equipment or equipment rental and contracts for services. Also included are the allowed participant costs of books, materials, travel, room and board and stipends.

The institution was allowed, in this case, a flat rate of 8 percent for F&A cost recovery. These funds are given to the institution to defray such fixed costs as accounting, payroll, purchasing, administration, plant operations and maintenance,

75

depreciation of buildings and equipment, and use of student services, such as admissions or registrar's offices.

The F&A cost components are facilities: buildings and improvements, interest, equipment, operations and maintenance, library, and administration: general administration, departmental administration, sponsored projects administration and student services administration. The percentage breakdown differs from one F&A agreement to another, but on the average about 51 percent of the recovery goes to administration, with the other 49 percent to facilities.

An institution or school district does not simply "fix" its own rate. The rates are established through a complex audit process that is described in OMB Circular A-21 (www.whitehouse.gov/omb/rewrite/circulars/a021/a021.html). Often the U.S. Department of Health and Human Services or the Department of Defense will establish a rate or, more usually, a series of rates that apply to different sectors or locations where the project takes place. For universities, these rates range from about 30 to 80 percent. Private contractors can go as high as 120 percent.

In the budget illustrated in Appendix A, the rate is a maximum of 8 percent, even though the institution's actual negotiated rate is 55 percent on-campus and 26 percent off-campus. In this example, it means that, even though the institution has a legal 55 percent F&A factor, the funding agency will only allow an 8 percent allowance. As a grant-writer, you do specify the legal F&A cost rate. Thus the funding agency or its program officer has knowledge of what the entitlement really is.

The basic rationale and logic supporting F&A costs is that by contracting for selected services or products it is more economical for the federal government to pay some administrative fee than it would be for the Feds to build the laboratory, staff it, pay for its maintenance and conduct the project.

Additionally, educational organizations do have basic missions. When grants are awarded, the sponsored projects remove some space, time, equipment and human resources from the institution's primary mission. Thus, the F&A cost rate is established to pay for costs not directly identified in the proposal, but those indirectly benefiting the project. For example, some simple ones are local telephone calls, utilities for project offices, janitorial services, support to operate that mass spectrometer, safety services and many other regular functions.

In research universities, it is easy to identify the hundreds of people employed due to the increased workload caused by awarded grants and contracts. Somebody has to do the paperwork. How the F&A costs are spent or distributed is determined, in part, by OMB Circular A-21 and institutional policy. For example, enlightened administrators draft policies that allow some of the F&A costs to be returned to principal investigators as "seed money" for future activities. One university allocates 20 percent to departments and 10 percent to colleges. The remaining 70 percent is subdivided between actual operational costs, general fund obligations, international programs, research parks, employee benefits, carry-forward funds and the graduate school.

In school districts, the F&A amount is very small, usually 4–5 percent, but almost never exceeds an 8 or 10 percent maximum. So, at a major research university, a $1 million direct cost grant could bring $450,000 or more to the F&A cost column. Don't worry: those allowed F&A costs are a part of doing business and your proposal will not be rejected because of those added costs. And, yes, federal auditors do review the annual F&A costs reported to the Feds (but seldom revealed to the public).

Much more could be written about F&A costs, but this gives you an awareness of that seemingly mysterious factor.

Again, we must also note that most non-profit foundations do not fund F&A costs. If it is not clearly stated in the foundation guidelines, do contact their respective program officers to make an inquiry.

OTHER BUDGETING CONSIDERATIONS

Carefully read the guidelines concerning what is allowed and disallowed for any specific agency or foundation. But what if you want to bring in your favorite aunt as a consultant? Her daily pay rate will differ from that of the other program staff. The federal consultant rate is $513 per day from the U.S. Department of Education for rehabilitation training grants; U.S. Department of Justice is $450 per day; NSF is $521 per day; some U.S. Department of State programs have a maximum of $300 per day. Other federal departments have no specific limit. OMB A-21 does not impose a specific limit on consulting costs. It does require such costs to be as reasonable as possible for the proposed work. Of course, travel and per diem would also be paid at your institutional policy rate. No, your aunt cannot fly super-first-class-deluxe, contrary to public opinion. All consultants must be mentioned in the narrative and the role they will play. They cannot simply be introduced with a budget line.

Cost-sharing was discussed in Principle 11. However, one great source of cost-sharing is to use the difference between the negotiated and actual F&A rate allowed by an agency. For example, in most cases, the U.S. Department of Education allows an 8 percent maximum for indirect costs. Assume that your organization has an established rate of 50 percent. The cost-sharing is the difference or 42 percent. If you received a $100,000 grant plus 8 percent for F&A costs, you use the difference or $42,000 as in-kind cost-sharing. What that means is that the receiving institution may then show that $42,000 as its share of cost-sharing. It's perfectly legitimate.

However, a word of caution is needed when making the calculations. If you use "F&A cost waivers," as it is officially called—that is, the institution will allow a lesser amount for the F&A costs—then proposal budget justification must show an elaboration of the base upon which the reduced rate is applied. This specified base generally is the "total direct cost" and includes all direct costs except those specifically exempted within the guidelines. The "full" rates of most institutions are based on "modified total direct cost," which contains a far more comprehensive list of direct cost exclusions. Hence, in computing F&A costs, which have been waived, you must compute the full federally allowable F&A cost and subtract out the F&A cost allowable rather than applying a "net" rate. Absolutely discuss this method at great length with your own fiscal officer so that no errors are computed and the budget justification is clearly stated.

Dissemination of results is an allowable direct cost. This was mentioned in Principle 9. However, if you have a large developmental grant and you want to "get the word out to cosmopolites," then a sizable amount of the direct costs could be allocated to this feature. During the curriculum development era of the National Science Foundation, for five major projects the NSF awarded $20.5 million for curriculum development costs and $22.9 million for implementation (dissemination) costs (see Orlich, 1987, p. 20). Without implementation or dissemination activities, diffusion of ideas or projects would be limited. In business, these activities are called "advertising."

Yes, participants can be paid an honorarium for attending workshops, institutes or in-service programs. Again, the guidelines will provide details.

Just as the project gets under way, you discover that one line item has more than you need and another has much less. Now what? Call the program officer. Explain the situation. In nearly all cases, you will be allowed to make reasonable shifts between budget lines. Some agencies even allow you a 10 percent shift in any category without requesting permission. However, if some major change is required, you may have to submit a new budget for agency approval.

In many instances, you'll be called by the program officer to cut the budget by some percentage. So, be prepared with a contingency plan and a reduced scope of work.

The best way to learn about budgeting is to create one, although our model in Appendix A will give you a good idea how they are constructed. Before closing, remember that you must have your budget approved by your own institutional budget office prior to the full proposal's submission. A budget checklist follows that will help you critique your fiscal plan.

CHECKLIST: Budget

1. Budget lines coincide with narrative.

2. All budget activities are mentioned in the proposal.

3. Accurate data are presented.

4. Institutional policies guide specific allocations.

5. Uniform percentage changes are used for long-term budgets.

6. The guidelines are meticulously followed.

7. Your program officer first approves any fiscal deviations.

8. Your budget office approved the plan.

9. Be prepared to reduce the budget when the proposal is accepted.

10. Determine whether any reduced final budget is adequate to conduct the project.

11. If you don't ask, then you will not receive.

Chapter 7

Preparing Research Proposals

CHAPTER SUMMARY

- Research Programs
- Testing Hypotheses
- Various Methodologies — Non-Experimental Designs
- Experimental Designs
- Reviews and Certifications
- Detailed Evaluation Checklist for Research Proposals

There are thousands of published and currently cataloged books for circulation addressing the topics of research, research design, research methods and research theory. That wealth of resources would make it amply redundant on our part to discuss all the aspects relating to the topic. However, a book on grant proposal writing isn't complete without some guidelines. The perspective in this chapter is that research grants tend to go to individuals or groups who have a fully established research program. Let us examine the implications for "extramural" funding.

RESEARCH PROGRAMS

Well-funded scientific researchers all have long-term, well-established research programs. These researchers have an agenda of areas on which they devote their time and energy. In most cases, their laboratories are equipped specifically to fit the type of research they conduct. They don't skip from opportunistic topics or faddish issues to another. Top researchers establish a program based on tough problems for which no reasonable description or solution has been published. They carefully select significant problems. These problems are well supported by theory or predictive and supportive hypotheses. Experiments are carefully designed. In most cases, research scientists spend one or two years working in postdoctoral fellowships. The research internship for these individuals is grueling.

One needs to think about the long-range viability of a research program. Why? Because, to obtain competitive funds at the national level, you must demonstrate some success. If you seek research grants from the National Institutes of Health (NIH) or the National Science Foundation (NSF), you already have to have published successful studies. Note how the "P" word has been used. Research means publishing, disseminating, giving refereed papers; but, above all—publishing!

To begin a research program, do obtain those small grants often offered as "seed or start-up money" in universities or in forward-looking school districts. You begin a research program, gain some success, chalk up a few victories, establish a set of credible publications, and you are ready for the "big ones."

TESTING HYPOTHESES

Successful research proposals incorporate all the elements previously discussed: problem, hypotheses, objectives, procedures where specific protocols are presented, subjects, personnel, equipment, travel, stipends and facilities and administrative costs (F&A, also referred to as indirect costs). Funded researchers carefully design their studies, but they always have specific objectives. Refer to Chapters 1 and 4 for those earlier comments. More importantly, long-range research problems test hypotheses.

Research Hypotheses

A research hypothesis is a statement that may concern cause and effect relationships. In most scientific groups, some specific hypothesis will be tested for verification or shown not to be valid. Often it is written using the logic of the "if–then" syllogism. Scientific fields have literally thousands of research hypotheses. In the social-behavioral sciences the research hypothesis may not be as well specified. In most cases, few faculty actually can state a research hypothesis that may have been inferred from empirical studies. Hypotheses are only as good as their ability to predict the probability of future actions or consequences to occur. That is why there are so few in the social-behavioral sciences and education.

Null Hypotheses

To determine if a hypothesis is testable in statistical terms, it is usually stated in the *null* form. The null hypothesis is a statement, which asserts that differences between groups will be due to chance, not the experimental statements:

> There is no significant difference in the level of adults with high IQ and those of low IQ.

This form of the null hypothesis means that no significant differences will be observed between post-test results of the two groups. If the data show no significant differences, then we "tentatively accept the research hypothesis." That is, there will be no statistical differences. If, however, one treatment group shows a statistical difference over the other group, then we "do not accept the null hypothesis." By not accepting the null hypothesis, the research hypothesis is accepted.

Null hypotheses are usually stated in the objectives or purpose section of the proposal. One sequence of topics could be:

1. Purpose of Study
2. Statement of Objectives
3. Research Hypotheses
4. Null Hypotheses
5. Acceptable Level of Statistical Significance
6. Review of Literature

The researcher selects the level of statistical significance at which the null hypotheses will not be accepted. If one were willing to accept results that could be due to chance alone 5 times out of 100, then the researcher would specify the .05 or .01 levels of statistical significance. The level of statistical significance is established before the study is conducted, not after. We already discussed using the effect size in Chapter 5, which in many cases is more meaningful and reliable than the tests of significance.

You should refer to any of the standard textbooks on statistical methods or research methods to seek elaboration on hypotheses testing. Our intent is to present an introduction to the topic as it pertains to proposal writing so that you may realize some of the details that affect the way you prepare a research proposal. We do imply that data will be generated of some nature. As a grant-writer, you need to establish the most meaningful tests for significance. This illustrates to the program officer and review panel members that chance is not a given.

Whether or not the non-acceptance of the null hypothesis is relevant to your area of research is, of course, another question. As an example the field of educational research has some evidence to show the triviality of many proposed research or null hypotheses. Unfortunately, most education researchers do not adequately control their experiments to allow a major generalization.

The single criterion on which a research hypothesis rests is "Can the hypothesis be empirically tested?" In scientific research, the experiment may well be the best technique by which to settle educational arguments. Of course, these experiments must meet the rigors of accepted methodology. In the social sciences, the subjects are not always as controllable as are physical objects, and thereby creating "messy" conditions or less than desirable controls.

VARIOUS METHODOLOGIES—NON-EXPERIMENTAL DESIGNS

There are several different types of methodologies that can accomplish a set of objectives. Each of the types listed below will be expanded briefly. In general, there are:

1. Surveys
2. Curriculum Development Projects
3. Staff Development Projects
4. Case or Qualitative Studies
5. Experimental Designs

Surveys

A frequently used methodology is the survey. Surveys are used to collect data about some specific trait or to obtain opinions concerning a set of concepts, ideas or programs. The survey basically comprises: (1) a set of objectives; (2) instruments, i.e., questionnaires or personal interview schedules; and (3) a sample of respondents. The most important part of the survey is the preparation of the data-collecting instrument. And, to conduct longitudinal studies, you need some testable hypotheses.

The sample may be selected by polling the entire population, e.g., teachers in a state, or by choosing a non-biased sample on a random basis. In some cases, a stratified random sample is chosen. The latter technique is used to insure representation from various subgroups of the population. Whatever sampling plan is used, it should be written in detail identifying who will be sampled, how the sample was established and why the techniques are being used.

Curriculum Development Projects

A very commonly funded educationally related "research" activity for K-12 and higher education educators stems around the production of needed courses, units or modules. Curriculum development goes beyond the mere formulation of a course of study. A curriculum study design is normally composed of a statement of objectives, description of methodology, scope and sequence of learning experiences, description of content and specification of procedures for evaluating the effectiveness of the curriculum.

Objectives should be stated concisely in terms of student learning and, perhaps, behaviors and translated into criteria against which the curriculum is to be evaluated. Recent advances in subject matter and learning theory should be reviewed as needed. The proposal should stress investigative or experimental activities rather than program implementation. The project should be innovative for the investigator undertaking it and should hold promise for contributing to curriculum improvement in other settings, i.e., is transportable or generalizable.

Curriculum activities generally fall within the areas of development or validation, or a combination of the two. A small project might be designed to create or to validate selected curriculum materials or methods as part of a larger curriculum effort. In unusual cases, a study could meet the requirements of a total curriculum effort in a specifically limited curriculum area.

When the research is primarily *development* of curriculum, the proposal should:

1. Describe the theoretical background, related research and bases by which new types of student experiences will relate to the objectives of instruction.
2. Designate which curriculum design areas are involved and reflect knowledge of previous work in the area.
3. Illustrate the process or procedure to be used, giving attention to how the present curriculum will be improved.

Curriculum development usually leads to the production of a "product" on completion of the project. The product may be a simulation, book, learning module, multimedia device, a set of methods for instruction or a new degree program. The procedures for curriculum development projects should specify the form of the final product. Hint: In these projects, work with a publishing company as a cooperating partner or a state board of higher education. This assures dissemination.

When the research is primarily *validation* of curriculum products or processes, the proposal should:

1. Delineate the area of curriculum design under investigation.
2. Identify the relevant variables designated for study and the procedures for determining the effects of these variables.
3. Describe the population involved, the data to be gathered and the instruments to be used.

The rationale for curriculum validation projects is to determine the appropriateness of curricula in different environments. Usually, one desires to know if a curriculum will achieve its intended ends with groups of students who were not involved in the initial development of the curriculum. As "integrated curricula" become an accepted part of the curriculum, several validation studies will need to be conducted to determine the efficacy of the curriculum materials prior to large-scale adoptions. Such research will reduce the chances of the classic blunder of the Physical Science Study Committee (PSSC), which developed a rigorous high school physics curriculum in the early 1960s. The PSSC was designed for the very best high school students. But guess who was convinced to use it? Right, all high school physics teachers. You didn't need the Enrico Fermi Award to predict the almost total collapse of high school physics enrollments because of this type of product dissemination and lack of curriculum validation by a group who should have been more empirically oriented. If materials do not teach well or the students incur great learning difficulties, the materials simply are not working. (Of course, this assumes the instructors' behaviors are appropriate to the curriculum and prerequisite learning skills by the students.) Curriculum validation projects are very essential to the success for the total educational program—and to the success of the students.

Professional Development Projects

Professional development or in-service education is very much a part of research and development. Regardless of what has been written about outcomes or institutional reform and a myriad of other techniques, in the last analysis, the staff (teachers/instructors/faculty) implements innovations! An aware and sensitive staff is the basis for change.

The preparation of a professional development project is almost identical to that of a curriculum project, *except* the emphasis is placed on the preparation of a selected individual's with a set of competencies, instructional methods, curriculum techniques or program skills.

Case Studies

Researchers in many of the different social science disciplines and many others have long used case studies. The case study is an attempt to provide an objective description of what takes place (behaviors, conditions, attitudes) with usually no attempt to manipulate variables. (Medical case studies are, of course, an exception.) To manipulate variables means that the independent variable is systematically applied to the subjects in question. Qualitative studies and action research studies are all very similar. (Purists will scorn us for such a cavalier treatment.)

85

These studies are helpful for fact-finding and for describing changes that may take place in individuals, organizations or instructional techniques. When using these methodologies, you must be cautious that personal bias or systematic observational bias is not inadvertently built into the design. These methods study a detailed examination of one subject, instruction or community considered as a unit. The drawing of inferences or conclusions from them requires a great deal of caution. Some researchers argue that no generalizations may be made. However, as grounded theory is generated, the statements may be converted into testable hypotheses.

This genre of studies is most helpful in identifying possible leads that might isolate critical independent or dependent variables. The latter could then be tested through experimental studies.

EXPERIMENTAL DESIGNS

The previous methodologies typically lack the use of control and experimental groups, wherein the experimental group receives the manipulated or independent variable. As one approaches "true" experimental research, there is need for careful control and application of the independent variable. To be certain that some outcome or trait is caused by the experimental treatment, there is need for large groups of subjects or students. This section will not attempt to describe all experimental designs, since there are many books on that topic. What will be presented are a few basic tenets of experimental design that can be used effectively by any researcher who desires to control or manipulate one independent variable or set of variables.

Typically, variables are classified as *independent* and *dependent*. The *independent variable* is some characteristic, behavior, procedure or curriculum that ought to be associated with some effect or *dependent variable*. The classic experiment with Pavlov's dog might be called to mind. Remember, Pavlov rang a bell each time the dog was fed. Ultimately, Pavlov could ring the bell (independent variable) and the dog would salivate (dependent variable) without being fed.

In all experimental designs, it is usually assumed that if some independent variable occurs, it will be associated with another characteristic or observable event—the dependent variable. It must be cautioned that specified conditions are needed to produce such a relationship. A few years ago, a study was conducted in which the researcher concluded there was a somewhat high probability of a student's owning a car and receiving relatively poor grades. The independent variable was owning a car, while receiving relatively poor grades was the dependent variable. Now, to test this hypothesis, one ought to predict success in high school as measured by grades and automobile ownership. The only problem is that the correlation is so low that the predictions are no better than chance alone.

Why the discrepancy? There are too many other independent variables associated with auto ownership and grades. Further, it must be cautioned that correlations rarely, if ever, determine cause and effect.

As you plan for research experiments, the following factors must be considered:

1. Instrumentation (Tests or Measurement Devices)
2. Subjects
3. Control and Experimental Groups
4. Independent Variable (the Treatment)
5. Post-Testing
6. Analysis of Results

Instrumentation

If the subjects are truly *randomly* assigned to experimental and control groups, a pre-test is not always necessary because any differences between groups on the post-test will reflect *changes* produced by the introduction of the independent variable, i.e., the experimental treatment.

Instruments may be adapted from those already published. However, if you do adapt an instrument that has a copyright, be sure to seek written permission from the publisher *before* you alter the instrument. If not, you may be the subject of litigation.

Where explicit outcomes are specified, criterion measures may be converted into the instruments and used collectively to form the standards by which achievement will be determined.

Regardless of the approach to be used, reliable and valid tests should be used. The researcher ought to know for whom the tests were designed and how accurately they predict traits for the intended group.

Subjects

The subjects used in an experiment should all be rather homogeneous in selected traits. You need to be sure that all subjects exhibit approximately the same trait prior to applying the independent variable with the experimental group. However, if the sample of subjects is randomly selected and randomly assigned to the control and experimental groups, the variability of traits will probably not affect the outcome. By using randomization, the researcher will avoid inadvertently introduced bias. The results from replicated random group experiments are usually more generalizable than are those where extensive statistical manipulations must be performed to equalize the groups.

The selection of subjects must be done without building in a bias, which will favor your treatment group. For example, it would be very unfair to match

87

15-year-old boys against 15-year-old girls on some skill, which required physical strength. But, one might match them on some manual dexterity program.

One last caution about the use of human subjects in experimental studies is needed. According to federal regulations adopted by the U.S. Department of Health and Human Services, no human subject may be exposed to experimentation that could cause physical or psychological harm. Researchers who desire to study rather sensitive issues, such as sexual habits, religion, family interactions or personal habits, may find their proposals flatly rejected. We will amplify this topic later in the chapter.

Control and Experimental Groups

Once the sample of the subjects has been defined, they ought to be randomly assigned to the treatment groups: the control group has no independent variable administered, while the experimental group receives the independent variable.

Participants or, as they are called in design, "the subjects" should be randomly selected for groups. Random means exactly that. The most random method of selection is to place the names of all subjects in a "hat," thoroughly mix them and draw one name alternatively for the control and experimental group. Also, software has been developed that will randomly select the subjects for creating the groups once the subjects' names are entered into a database.

In higher education, there are studies where an entire class can be randomly selected by a person independent from the study who determines which classes will act as experimental and which will act as control. The instructors would also be assigned to those classes in the same random manner. Such a selection assures the elimination of bias.

Independent Variable

The independent variable would be administered to the experimental group. This would be the group, for example, to receive instruction in math via computer or in the classroom.

The control group receives the same instruction, with the exception of the independent variable treatment.

This is difficult to achieve in some environments, since students frequently interact. Thus, there is a chance that your experimental group may exhibit the "Hawthorne effect." This means that, since they know that they are subjects for an experiment, they may act differently than they normally would in the same situation. This effect can be controlled by using randomly selected groups from different schools, or by giving the control group something different to do: a placebo. In this manner, all groups will think that they are doing something unique. The best method to counteract the Hawthorne effect is not to tell any of the subjects that they are in some "new" program, or that they are in some experiment. Make it "business as usual" for all groups.

It is essential that the researcher carefully control the independent variable treatment. This will lessen chances for the occurrence of contamination in either group.

Post-Testing

In some designs, there is only one pre-test and one post-test. This is very unfortunate since project success is contingent on only one student performance—the post-test. We would like to suggest that a series of "performance checks" be made through the duration of the experiment via formative evaluations that are specifically designed to monitor the project. This means a systematic assessment or test at each phase of the experiment should be made. From the series of formative measures, data may be derived which can be compared to the baseline for all groups and for different time intervals. (See Hattie, 2009, for an excellent treatment on this topic.)

The post-test or summative test is the final testing of all groups. The post-test should be accomplished at the same time for all groups to avoid any contamination of data.

An analysis of the data, test results or comparisons between or among groups is essential. In most cases, parametric statistical tests will be used. These tests must be planned in advance so that the collected data will meet the assumption of each specific statistical analysis. Almost all school districts and institutions of higher education have evaluation specialists. Identify these individuals before the project is funded so that data analysis may be conducted easily through electronic data-processing equipment.

When designing the project, the above elements should be addressed. If your research yields interesting results, there should be a replication or duplication at other sites or your laboratory to determine the efficacy of the independent variable. That may imply no end to being a "grant-seeker."

The above may sound overpowering to the novice who has a "good idea." But remember, ideas are not funded—*procedures are!* Collectively, the procedures, hypotheses and objectives must support each other. This does not mean curbing your creativity. It simply means that your creative efforts will be logically and systematically developed so they may be funded.

REVIEWS AND CERTIFICATIONS

You have just spent the past eight weeks developing and crafting your research proposal. Three internal reviewers gave you great feedback and encouragement. Then, the director of research said, "Where are your certifications and assurances?" Puzzled, you ask, "What . . . ?" Certifications and assurances are federally mandated legal points that must be addressed positively or your proposal may be rejected.

As of this writing, there are 12 separate assurances or certificates that you must prepare. The most critical is the protection of human subjects, which will be expanded in the next section. The other concerns:

- Treatment of Vertebrate Animals
- Claim for Inventions and Patents
- Freedom from Previous Debarment or Suspension
- Maintenance of a Drug-Free Workplace
- Disclaimer from Lobbying
- No Delinquent Federal Debts (for You or Your Institution)
- Policies Regarding Misconduct in Science
- Export Control
- Civil Rights Assurance
- Non-Discrimination against Handicapped Individuals
- No Sex Discrimination
- No Age Discrimination

Certificates for each of these must be prepared showing that you meet the criteria that each certificate requires. You may go on-line and seek Office of Management and Budget Circular A-95 and 45 Catalog of Federal Regulations 46, which are very easy-to-use notations on certificates and assurances. Additionally, if your research uses radioactive materials, recombinant DNA, carcinogenic chemicals or any hazardous items, special care must be noted in the proposal.

Human Subject Review

This review is a must if any human subjects will be used in your anticipated research. It usually follows the procedures section that addresses human subjects. As you can quickly infer, these requirements came about over the past several years as unethical or fraudulent claims were made. Every time some researcher goes beyond the ethics or morals of the community, a new assurance is added. The most acclaimed case is, of course, the infamous Tuskegee case that was found to be a misguided syphilis study instituted by the U.S. Public Health Service in the 1930s. The news broke in July of 1972 that 600 black men had been involved in a 40-year non-treatment study—even though cures were available. Congress reacted quickly with the passage of the National Research Act (PL 93-348), signed into law on July 12, 1974. The act established criteria for use of human-related research.

The discussions and regulations on treatment of humans are voluminous. We will give just an orientation so that you will be able to check with your "Institutional Review Board," or IRB. Every research university, institution or hospital has an IRB. The board is charged to review *all* research proposals that involve humans. A proposal will not be considered for funding nor permitted to be completed without funding if the IRB concludes that there are risks to the human subjects that outweigh the gains in knowledge. The risks may be physical, emotional, psychological, discomfort, stress or invasion of privacy. Further, if sensitive issues are being addressed, e.g., sexual experiences, drug or alcohol use or collection of data that may damage the subject's financial standing, employability or reputation, then the research must describe the risks and how the risk will be handled or compensated.

One key element is the use of "informed consent." All subjects must be told of potential risks and that a subject may withdraw from the study at any time without fear of reprisal. Further, if minors are involved, parental consent must be obtained.

For research projects where there is no or minimal risk, such as most training or curriculum development projects, the IRB review may be expedited. If you use a questionnaire, the IRB may examine only those questions that are considered "sensitive." With self-administered questionnaires, the general reaction is "implied consent." That is, if the respondent sends back the completed questionnaire, then that action is inferred to be "implied consent." You must not identify any respondent by name, as that would be considered an invasion of privacy. If a study will require follow-up data from the subjects so their names and other contact information is recorded, a researcher needs to work with their local IRB to meet the needed privacy parameters.

Other Concerns

Depending on your own institutional policy, you might be asked to certify that certain conditions are or are not required. For example:

- Ample Space
- Radiation Safety
- Security Clearances
- Special Laboratory Services
- Commitment for Matching Funds or Cost-Sharing
- Regional Clearinghouse Approval
- Conflict of Interest
- Outside Contractors
- Extra Library Support
- Mainframe Computer Uses

- Special Equipment Considerations
- Foreign Travel

The above 12 considerations are often required by the institution to protect itself. You can imagine a university president's surprise to learn that a $100,000 research grant was awarded to a professor, with the contingency that the school would construct a $2 million laboratory in which to conduct the study. Or equipment funded from a grant arrives on campus to be installed. Those responsible very quickly realize that no pre-planning was done with facilities operations before submitting the proposal because the equipment is too big to get inside the building, which will now require a major overall so to be placed in the researcher's laboratory.

The above are just a few critical items that you need to consider as you prepare your timelines for submission of the proposal and accomplishment of the needed assurances and certificates without becoming stressed. It is all part of the success that goes with carefully developed and crafted proposals funded research.

A checklist closes the chapter with a handy guide by which to evaluate your proposal in detail before you submit it.

CHECKLIST: Detailed Evaluation Checklist for Research Proposals

NA = Not Applicable
1 = Very Inadequate (VI)
2 = Inadequate (I)
3 = Adequate (A)
4 = Very Adequate (VA)

NEEDS OR PROBLEM		SCORES			
		VI	I	A	VA
1. Needs for project are clearly stated.		1	2	3	4
2. Needs for project are clearly documented.		1	2	3	4
3. Problem is significant.		1	2	3	4
OBJECTIVES					
4. Objectives are clearly stated.		1	2	3	4
5. Objectives are related to identified needs.		1	2	3	4
6. Objectives are measurable or observable.	NA	1	2	3	4
PROCEDURES					
7. Limitations of the project are stated.	NA	1	2	3	4
8. Important terms are defined.	NA	1	2	3	4

9. Procedures to conduct project are described explicitly.		1	2	3	4
10. Procedures design is appropriate to accomplish objectives.		1	2	3	4
11. Procedures are appropriately sequenced.		1	2	3	4
12. Population of study is described.	NA	1	2	3	4
13. Method of identifying population is appropriate.	NA	1	2	3	4
14. Data-gathering methods or procedures are described.	NA	1	2	3	4
15. Data-gathering methods or procedures are appropriate.	NA	1	2	3	4
16. Review of literature is appropriate.	NA	1	2	3	4

EVALUATION

17. Evaluation design or data analysis is specified.	NA	1	2	3	4
18. Evaluation is oriented toward project objectives.	NA	1	2	3	4

ASSURANCES

19. Human subject assurances clearly identified.	NA	1	2	3	4
20. Animal care specified.	NA	1	2	3	4
21. Any hazard is clearly discussed.	NA	1	2	3	4
22. Informed consent form appended.	NA	1	2	3	4
23. IRB approval.	NA	1	2	3	4
24. Budget is adequate or realistic to conduct project.		1	2	3	4
25. Proposal is explicitly written.		1	2	3	4
26. Proposal is logically organized.		1	2	3	4
27. Proposal addresses societal impact.		1	2	3	4

GENERAL

28. Proposal displays unbiased style.		1	2	3	4
29. Project is transportable or results publishable.		1	2	3	4
30. Project is socially or educationally significant.		1	2	3	4
31. The proposal was internally reviewed.		1	2	3	4

32. The probability for funding the proposal as now written is:

_____

_____

Chapter 8

Strategies for Classroom Support

CHAPTER SUMMARY

- Seeking a Solution and Locating a Funder
- Making Time to Craft Your Proposal
- Scholarships, Sabbaticals and Travel Grants
- Being Recognized—Awards
- Initiating a Support Network
- Repeating Your Success
- Strategies for Classroom Support Checklist

As a classroom teacher, community college instructor or university professor, you may not be interested in writing large complex grants. Perhaps you would simply like to obtain a few dollars for something that helps improve the instructional and learning processes. This chapter is designed for your immediate application.

The strategies for obtaining additional classroom resources for instruction are very similar to those discussed already. However, the scale of the project is reduced, as will be the physical size of your proposal or request for extramural funds. The first step in this process is to write out the observed needs. Is that map of the USSR 44 years out of date, but too expensive to replace with your school district's almost non-existent instructional materials fund? Would a small portable laptop computer help students collect data when they are doing field research? Could a digital camera help your students capture scenes that enhance student-produced web pages? Would your art appreciation class be more realistic if you had a 250-slide set of classic paintings for class discussion? Notice how each of these instructional items is very specific to a classroom condition? At this point, stop reading and jot down three or four items of equipment that would make your instructional efforts just a little more efficacious.

SEEKING A SOLUTION AND LOCATING A FUNDER

There may be other needs that are more nonmaterial, that is, the resources you need are more of a social benefit to students. One example is a project called "Kids First," sponsored by the North Central Education Service District in Wenatchee, Washington. In this program, a fund has been accumulated via donations to provide some direct benefit to a child. Let us say that you observe a child from a socio-economically poor family who appears to need glasses. You write this condition in a short letter-like proposal stating the need you observed and the solution to address it. If your school district doesn't have a program such as "Kids First," then you can try the same strategy with one of the local service clubs— Lions, Rotary, Kiwanis, Soroptimists. These clubs have a long history of helping children, but somebody has to alert them. And that's where you come in with your knowledge in crafting a small-scale grant proposal that helps just one student.

We already mentioned local service clubs as potential sources for small-scale proposals. Nearly all telephone, electric and gas utility companies provide some assistance to schools and community non-profit organizations. In most cases, these efforts are conducted through the public relations office or some specific unit. A letter of inquiry to your local utility company is your start. Before you fire off that letter, first obtain the exact name of the appropriate contact person. This is no place for some impersonal "to whom it may concern" letter, as it may end up in the trash bin.

Regional banks are also excellent sources for small grants. Banks often sponsor foundations; you might make an appointment with the local branch manager to inquire if the bank has a non-profit foundation. Again, as with other businesses, if no foundation is established, they may fund out of the public relations department. Most of your local business establishments are "touched" for ads to be placed in your public relations materials. So these groups are best left out of the small-scale proposal process as "they are already giving at the office."

To identify potential funding sources is a time-consuming task. You might inquire through your school's parent–teacher association if some parent or small group might take on the task of identifying community resource providers. This tactic expands the horizon for finding potential funds or materials and also gets parents involved in helping to improve instruction. If you teach in a large city or community, it might even have a community foundation. At most colleges and universities, there are organized parent groups that will fund activities, brick-and-mortar projects and other needs that directly enhance their children's experience in higher education or their road toward graduating. The secret to success is to create a network of helpers in the process.

Community colleges and universities usually have a centralized office of grant and research development. Most even have a 501(c)(3) non-profit foundation. Make inquiries of these groups about possible funding sources or avenues for obtaining funds.

MAKING TIME TO CRAFT YOUR PROPOSAL

By now, you realize that writing a proposal is a labor-intensive task. How does a busy person ever find time to write a proposal? The ideal would be to get some release time during the day to work on your proposal. You might ask the principal to take your class for a couple of hours or your department chair for some release time, so you can begin composing your proposal. This method also keeps the principal or chair in the network.

Another way might be to ask one of your colleagues to manage your class when some large-group activity takes place. Many times at the college of university level, the instructor/faculty member will assign an out-of-class project like doing research in the library or group project meetings during regular class time. This gives you a chance to create a page or two. Maybe even that letter of intent.

A novel method that is used in higher education is to discuss your idea with a class that has an interest in your proposal topic. And then as a writing experience they all pitch in to draft a preliminary proposal. Their comments will be very genuine and client-oriented for your needs; and many times the students can use the document for part of their writing portfolios.

Yet another method is to collaborate with another colleague who may have the same need. This means more time has to be allotted to coordinate with your colleague(s), but also a much stronger proposal that reflects more impact outcome.

Whether you are in the K-12 system or in higher education, you may have to take the proposal home and dedicate your time to it as you would if it was a batch of papers that needed to be corrected.

Finally, in many school systems teachers/instructors/faculty are required to prepare a "professional development plan." You could develop your plan to write one or two curriculum-oriented project proposals or to seek help in drafting a disciplinary related project.

Those in higher education do not have teaching loads like K-12 sector teachers. Thus, making time to seek funding and writing the proposals can be built into open-time hours. And, many times, requires instructors/faculty to do some homework also!

The most effective way is to make time every day, if possible at the same time. Identify what time of day is the best for you. Are you a morning person, an afternoon or evening person for being the most effective at whatever you are doing? Write for short periods of time (30 to 60 minutes). Put it away and come back to it the next day at the same time. Don't wait until two days before the proposal is due. Start early enough that there is no pressure on finishing and there is time for you and others to proof and edit the document.

SCHOLARSHIPS, SABBATICALS AND TRAVEL GRANTS

As a teacher or instructor, you have numerous opportunities to enhance your professional knowledge and skills. In the fields of mathematics and science, the number of scholarships for extended study or even for advanced degrees is vast. The National Science Foundation funds colleges and universities directly to conduct postgraduate studies for classroom teachers. These range from one-, two- or six-week single-focus, intensive workshops to fully funded master's degrees. The best source for locating these institutes or programs is through the National Science Teachers Association (NSTA) or the National Council of Teachers of Mathematics (NCTM). Both associations publish extensive lists in their publications.

The U.S. Department of Education publishes ENC materials from their new website, goENC.com. This is a subscription service that continues to offer the same timely, high-quality math and science resources you've come to expect from ENC. From professional development to lesson plans to web resources, it's all here. Learn how your school, school district, university or library can subscribe at goENC.com.

Several federally sponsored regional educational laboratories likewise advertise education projects that benefit teachers. For example, the North West Regional Educational Laboratory in Portland, Oregon sends out regular announcements via E-mail announcing various activities or teacher-oriented projects. The McREL Laboratory in Colorado publishes a great deal of instructionally related materials that benefit classroom teachers. All federal laboratories have extensive websites and can be accessed by the Internet. Research for Better Schools (RBS) in Philadelphia likewise provides opportunities for teachers. RBS is a private, non-profit educational organization funded primarily through grants and contracts from the U.S. Department of Education, the National Science Foundation, Mid-Atlantic state departments of education, institutions of higher education, foundations and school districts.

In a similar vein, educational programs are available for teachers of English, humanities and social studies. The respective national professional associations can help in the search for after-school, summer or even academic year programs. A letter of inquiry to a research university might just pay large dividends. Typically, the dean of the graduate school will have lists of funded teacher support programs.

For example, co-author Orlich participated in two master's degree programs as one of the course instructors. The first was an M.A. in chemistry where teachers were brought to campus for some courses, received videotaped classes during their school year, and then had a capstone summer research experience with a major

97

research laboratory. The pace was grueling, but all who competed received tidy stipends during the training and, at no cost to the teachers, an advanced degree. The second was as M.S. in biology with similar conditions.

Sabbatical leaves are typically awarded after seven to ten years of service with a school district. In higher education the time varies from five to seven years of full service as a tenure track or tenured person. Conducting research is usually one of the key reasons for requesting a sabbatical. Since policies differ so greatly, we will be generic. First obtain a set of your policies and guidelines. You will have to prepare a "plan" as part of your application. These plans are virtually identical to the proposal outlines already described. You should have a specific "need" to address and then be creative. Sabbatical leaves include curriculum development projects; preparation of course materials to meet state or national standards and even advanced education in some areas of need in your school or district. Often, you need a letter of support or endorsement from someone in the area in which you desire to do your sabbatical. Plan for these early so that all your needed documentation will be ready by the deadline. Relevant travel is often described in sabbatical plans. The key point is to be able to illustrate how your students, school and you will benefit. This takes practice, so begin the justification early in the drafting process.

Travel grants are usually related to attending professionally related state, regional, national or international conventions and conferences. The first priority goes to those who are presenting a paper or sessions. Now this is a problem because you need to plan at least two years in advance. The call for papers is often 9 to 12 months in advance of the actual conference. Thus, you need to apply simultaneously to the association to present a paper and to your institution for a travel grant that is contingent on having your paper accepted. Note in the last sentence, the term "contingent" was used. By using that term, you show the officials that you desire travel support, only if you are selected to participate in the conference. This illustrates responsibility on your part.

Your travel grant application should follow the established policies. If there are none, then prepare your request just like a grant proposal. Do extend the justification to show direct benefit to your students and school, plus volunteer to give a presentation to your colleagues about the conference highlights. Naturally, you'll need a detailed budget to include airfare, taxicabs, lodging, meals and registration. Try to be as exact in the budget request as is possible. Use exact numbers; do not round off your dollar figures. It's all a part of being fiscally prudent.

Now, you can have the conference pay for all or part of your way if you have some special talent and are willing to conduct either a pre- or post-conference workshop. You check with the association's convention coordinator for the guidelines. This is a novel way of showing your colleagues and administrators that you are taking that extra step to stretch the always-tight travel budget.

BEING RECOGNIZED—AWARDS

Teachers, by their disposition, tend to downplay their unique attributes or successes. In short, they do not like to "brag." (You'll not find such modesty among university professors.) How does one get recognized for exemplary teaching, service or administration? There are basically two ways: self-nomination and having another make the nomination. More than likely, you have seen all kinds of teacher recognition awards—National Teacher of the Year, Milken Teacher Awardees, State Teacher of the Year, Outstanding "_____" (fill in the blank). The first thing is to ask yourself is, "Do I fit the criteria for any of these awards?" If you think you do, then begin the self-nomination process. If you do not tell the sponsoring group about your success story, who will?

In many instances, you have to be nominated. Here is where you use a bit of tact, maybe even some politics, and ask someone else to nominate you. However, you can complete the application, provide the needed documentation and, if needed, the persons who you know will write strong letters of recommendation. That is all there is to it. Well, not exactly. You need to prepare a portfolio of your relevant activities, projects, professional contributions and even samples of newspaper clippings about your students who have been recognized. Keep an up-to-date vita. If you have pictures or video clips of you and your students in action, then keep them on file.

Do not be bashful about being recognized. The reason that associations, foundations and businesses recognize educators is because it is socially rewarding work. Being recognized for good work is good for morale and you'll even work harder after receiving the "plaque" to show you were worthy of the recognition. Oh, don't forget to notify the editor of the alumni magazine from your home institution of higher education. They enjoy telling other alumni of good deeds— so much for self-aggrandizement. Let us now get back to writing small grant proposals with some help.

INITIATING A SUPPORT NETWORK

Perhaps this section should be attached to one about finding time and energy to write grant proposals. But it is really a very distinct political and professional process. Proposal writing is a labor-intensive activity no matter how experienced one is in the craft. Being an instructor, you need to seek out colleagues and administrators who share your desire to be funded. Over some informal setting— coffee break, lunch—you discuss what kinds of grants you'd all be seeking. Then you discuss the various tasks that need to be done. These would include: (1) searching for sources, (2) preparing needs assessments and other supportive data, (3) drafting the initial draft, (4) preparing the budget, (5) designing the evaluation model, (6) obtaining necessary letters of endorsement, (7) preparing the physical manuscript, (8) editing and critiquing the proposal and (9) submitting the final application to the funder. If two or three colleagues can collaborate, then you have initiated a support network. It is that easy.

Depending on the support services that college, university or school district can offer, you might modify the scope of network activities. For example, if the district monitors funding sources, then one person can be the contact person and bring back a list of potential funders and other details. By working together and sharing in the reward process, you automatically increase the probability for success. Yes, two heads are better than one. And a word of caution: Do not wear your feelings on your shirtsleeves! Working collaboratively requires compromise. Your goal is to get the money and initiate a project. There is no need to feel offended because your favorite term or paragraph was deleted by a colleague when editing. Good luck!

REPEATING YOUR SUCCESS

Your efforts have been rewarded with a letter announcing the funding of your proposal. As the sign on the office door of a former superintendent of schools in Butte, Montana read, "Plan your work. Work your plan." Your proposal is now ready to be implemented. The various steps you outlined are all complete. But did you write a personal letter of thanks to the funder? Better yet, since the grant had some student benefit, let the students send a genuine letter or card thanking your funder for making the project a reality. Such an action is received most happily. Of course you want your school's information officer, if you have one, to notify the appropriate media in your town. Good school news is good news!

How do you repeat your initial success? Others are eager to fund worthwhile instructionally related projects. So, keep records relating to the proposal. These would include the needs assessment, the budget, the final evaluation results, and any newspaper clippings about the project. We personally prefer newspapers because they are physical and can be used to show other potential funders that you can do the job right.

What new condition do you and your network team members perceive? Perhaps you all would like to go for a bigger grant that has implications for multiple classrooms. In short, you play off your success with other proposals and you discuss how the first project leads to a new initiative. Review the guidelines of your initial funder to determine if or when you are eligible for either a renewal of your original project or for a new one. Your network team members should have also been busy locating potential funding sources, so you are well on the way to being a *grant-swinger*. Now let's examine a few models of small-scale proposals. Each of the models followed a distinct set of guidelines, therefore the differences in format.

MODEL 8.1: Letter of Intent for Hands-On Learning

The use of hands-on methods of teaching has long been proven successful to get across math concepts to students. The hands-on program we propose will help students make a connection with how math concepts are used in daily life and the students see, firsthand, the relationships of numbers to actual use.

Our program will use two methods of teaching math concepts. The first is the use of tile blocks to help students visualize math concepts. The blocks will be divided into containers appropriate to grade levels. The students experience a variety of challenges that will be solved using the blocks. Students will use the blocks to gain a sense of measurement concepts and work in teams to solve math problems while using the materials.

The second phase of the program will involve students using calculators appropriately. The calculators will be used specifically to show students how to apply their function in solving common math-related activities. This will give the student a comfort level when working with calculators and give students ideas of ways to incorporate the use of a calculator when trying to figure out math problems. We expect the use of the calculators and hands-on blocks to increase students' attention and comprehension of math concepts.

[The Letter of Intent in Model 8.1 was eventually funded for $1,000.]

MODEL 8.2: Letter of Intent for "Picture This"

Educators throughout our school enthusiastically support the effort to provide English as second language students with materials that enhance the students' ability to absorb the English language in a meaningful way.

Teachers will incorporate pictures and words into a variety of activities, practice sessions and projects that stimulate the interest of English as second language students as they begin to grasp the basic concepts of the English language no matter what age level the student is.

Keeping the students' interest will be the major focal point for the project. Through interest, students will better comprehend the educational aspects of the project.

The community has many students who are migrants. These students need to grasp, quickly, the English language. To do that, instructors will design a program by which students first identify a picture and then say what the picture is. Second, students match the picture to the corresponding English word, and spell the word on their own. Finally, the students use the pictures and word cards to put together sentences.

The instructors will also develop audiotapes that correspond with the appropriate picture card program in use to which the students can listen. This will help the students with pronunciation and aid students in developing sentence structure and syntax.

Games that students play will be used to get the students' attention and keep it. One game will involve tossing a coin or beanbag onto a stack of word cards. Once the object has landed, they name the word and use it in a sentence. Other games will include spelling tests using picture cards as word indicators.

Our evaluation will be to use a student interest inventory and a review of spelling and language progress.

[Model 8.2 was funded for $1,000.]

MODEL 8.3: Proposal of a School Arboretum Project: Goals and Objectives

1.a. Project description; educational need for such a project; purpose of the project; and the goals of the project.

Cave Creek School is in need of an outdoor arboretum to enhance our science curriculum. The arboretum would showcase only native plants on or around the school grounds. The arboretum will be an aesthetic and educational learning lab on our school grounds. The arboretum will help students become more aware of the richness of their immediate environment. The need to participate actively in an outdoor learning environment will be met with our proposed project. The purpose of the project is to provide a permanent hands-on field site that will supplement our science curriculum. The goal of our project is to design and construct a permanent field site arboretum and to begin to coordinate our science curriculum to take advantage of the educational resource.

1.b. Describe how the project will meet the educational need, as well as accomplishing the project's purpose and goals.

Our students will become observers of nature and will be responsible for identifying native plants in our area, bringing samples, if necessary, to transplant to the arboretum site and constructing signs that correctly label those plants. The construction and use of the arboretum will foster pride of workmanship and a feeling of ownership. By having a permanent outdoor arboretum, teachers and students can plan for interactive learning to take place in the natural environment.

2. Clearly state the projected educational outcomes of the project; what students will learn or be able to do as a result of participation in the project.

As a result of completion of this project, students will be able to lead a guided tour, sharing the information gained while creating the arboretum.

Students will be able to apply this knowledge to other areas in their environment and transfer the research skills to other areas of study.

After the project is completed, there will be a pride in ownership of having completed this permanent attraction for the school and future students.

3. **Explain how you will assess and evaluate the project's effectiveness in accomplishing the stated goals and realizing the projected educational outcomes.** We will assess the students' knowledge base by administering a pre- and post-test covering the information shared in the arboretum. For example, how many needles there are in a ponderosa pine bundle and describe how the needles of three different species are alike and different. These tests will be used to measure any gain in knowledge and changes in student attitude. We will also assess the completed arboretum for scientific accuracy and aesthetic qualities by using appropriate rubrics.

Upon completion of this activity, students will complete a written project, varying with the students' skill and grade level, analyzing how this project fits with other areas of their environment.

The students' pride of ownership will be assessed by observing how the students share their information during guided tours.

Project Description/Activities

1. **Describe the specific activities of the project in which students will be involved. Students will be in three aspects of this project.**

Team planning of the arboretum, including plant identification, route and station design, sign design and assessment of needed plants.

Construction of the path and signs, including transplanting and planting local native plants that are not already present in the arboretum route.

Leading or participating in student-led tours and participating in other curriculum activities.

2. **Describe what materials will be developed or used to enhance the student activities.**

The arboretum design, construction and future use will occur as a part of our botany and life science units. Initially, six to eight stations will be planned. Stations will include many varieties of native plant species. At each station, students will be asked site-specific questions about such things as plant density, types of plants growing at that site, and observations concerning the habitat. Students and teachers will develop guidebooks identifying and describing plants on the tour. The guidebooks can also be used as a supplement for self-guided or student-led tours. Sample guidebooks will be kept as a supplement for botany units, but future students will compile their own guidebook to keep.

3. **Explain the unique and innovative aspects of this project and how this uniqueness and innovation will enhance student learning.**

We try to present the life sciences in a way that centers on making connections in the immediate environment. This project not only will be designed by students, but also will be an ongoing part of our environmental science curriculum to which the school has already made a considerable commitment. For example, one area of the school grounds is used for bird watching and by planting different varieties of trees and shrubs students will be able to observe which plants particular birds prefer. This project also provides an opportunity for student, school board member, parent, teacher and school patron involvement in creating a permanent learning site.

Project Budget

Indicate exact costs for all aspects of your project for which you are seeking funds (items that have the potential for continuing impact on student learning).

item cost including tax

Gravel for Path $120/10 yd	$129.12
Pathway Edging 400' $1.00/ft.	$430.40
Sign Post, 10: 4x4x8 $1.06/ft.	$91.20
16' Cedar 1x12 Sign Material $1.80/ft.	$30.99
Marine Varnish for Signs	$15.06
100 Plant Markers	$73.00
Garden Supplies: Including a Shovel, Wheelbarrow	$215.20
TOTAL	**$984.97**

[Note: This proposal has approximately 1,140 words, excluding the budget. With a little expansion, it easily could be funded for $10,000.]

MODEL 8.4: Enhancing Learning in a Technology-Rich Environment

1. **How does your teaching help prepare students to meet the state standards.**

    To meet state standards, I align my objectives with the state standards and incorporate hands-on, open-ended investigations to promote problem solving and application of skills and concepts. We use group work to encourage develop of oral communication and social skills. Laboratory notebooks are used by students to record procedures and data, make predictions and justify answers, thus reinforcing writing skills. My students frequently ask, "How do you know that?" and "What is your evidence?" Portfolio assessments are used as a means of demonstrating mastery of unit objectives and ultimately specific standards. I purposefully teach non-fiction reading skills, regularly read aloud to my students, and allow weekly time for recreational reading. Students are taught research and report-writing methods.

2. **In a technology-rich classroom how do you or would you use technology to improve student learning?**

    I will create a homepage to post assignments, homework tasks and challenges. I will identify links to web-based resources. Students will use Excel spreadsheets to record data and create data tables, charts and graphs. Students will give PowerPoint reports. Appropriate on-line websites will be used to enhance the content being taught in my classroom. For example, frog dissecting could be first done on-line before actually working on a real frog. With a technology-rich classroom, I will be able to continue the learning process that is begun by our seventh grade science teachers who are both previous grant recipients. Awarding this grant for use in eighth grade science would provide an integrated continuity in science education in our building.

3. **How do you actively challenge yourself in your own learning to continue to develop and implement best instructional practices?**

   Lifelong learning is a personal "given." I love what I am doing, teaching eighth grade science. My greatest talent is my eagerness to seek out, learn and apply ideas that provide opportunities for my students to be actively involved in their learning. I was selected as one of 15 scholarship recipients for a Master of Science degree in Biology from Washington State University. After three years of hard work, this degree was awarded. The District Assessment Team, District Curriculum Team and District/Building Science Team are all active committees on which I serve. I chair the adoption committee in our building to find, evaluate and adopt a new science curriculum. I have attended many workshops and science teacher conferences to continually review and refresh my classroom skills. I welcome any new training that would help make me more effective as a teacher. My students will be direct beneficiaries of this grant.

[Model 8.4 was funded for $5,000.]

In Conclusion

This chapter focused on the teacher's instructional role in obtaining support for instructional activities. The checklist below is intended to help you in this endeavor.

CHECKLIST: Strategies for Classroom Support

- [ ] A list of classroom needs is established.
- [ ] Potential lists of funders are maintained.
- [ ] Model letters of intent are crafted and refined.
- [ ] The principal is made aware of the proposal.
- [ ] Professional journals and publications are systematically screened for potential scholarships for summer institutes.
- [ ] A professional development plan is outlined.
- [ ] Your vita is current.
- [ ] Professional recognition awards are examined for applicability.
- [ ] A support network is established.
- [ ] When funded, thank you letters and news releases are prepared.
- [ ] You maintain a file of all grant-related projects.

Chapter 9

Submitting the Proposal

CHAPTER SUMMARY

■ Planning the Details

■ Why Are Proposals Rejected?

■ The Review Process

■ Post-Script

■ Proposal Checklist for Technical Aspects

What a great feeling—joy and relief. The final draft of the proposal is completed. But it's still too soon to celebrate. There are some necessary details to which you must attend. Let's examine how the very successful grant-awardees complete the process.

PLANNING THE DETAILS

The first action is to take the entire proposal and carefully check it against the guidelines. Examine each criterion and sub-criterion of the guidelines. Did you address every item? If not, then make that addition right now. Keep in mind that the reviewers of your proposal will be given a set of evaluation checklists, similar to those illustrated throughout this book. Each criterion will be weighted with a set number of points, e.g., needs, 10 points; plan of operation, 40 points. To be successful, you must get as many points as possible and that is why you double-check every section in the guidelines or the published evaluation criteria.

Next, you review your headings. Do you use the same words as the guidelines? If not, go back and change them. For example, if the guidelines call the initial section "Significance of Project" and you have it labeled "Introduction," then some reviewers will miss that whole area and deduct all the points from your proposal because you did not specifically type out the words "Significance of the Project."

Now you double-check all the headings in your proposal so that they are identical to those used in the guidelines. Remember, it is funding you seek, not the creative writing of synonyms.

Check for parallel construction. When you made lists, did you use the same grammatical construction? That means using all infinitives or all gerunds when listing items. Refer to Chapter 3, where the lists of objectives were shown. Note how each list is parallel. By keeping lists parallel, it aids the reviewer and reduces chances for confusion.

Sure you have a spell checker, but have *you* carefully proofed the paper? Often, at this stage of the writing process, it is better to ask someone else to proof because you are "too close to it."

In the final typing of the manuscript, did you meet or exceed the page or character limitation? If not, okay, but if yes, go back and edit, reducing some sections. Foundations and agencies really mean it when they specify rigid page and character limitations. We know of a colleague who did not believe it and the entire set of proposals was returned with a little pre-printed card reminding him of the word count.

If you need your proposal package postmarked by a certain day and you might just be down to *that day*, then send the package via certified mail, receipt return. Certified mail is your only guarantee that the postmark is valid. (We'll discuss electronic submissions later in this chapter.)

Of course, if you must get the package to its proper destination by a set deadline day and hour, then you must plan ahead. Hint: We always give ourselves a two-day leeway just in case there might be a storm that closes the airport for 24 hours at the central collection point for one of our express service companies or overnight mail. In short, don't race to the deadline; allow some "slack."

Who had to sign the official cover sheet? If someone else must sign, be sure to notify that person's office and alert the person that you need a signature. The same action is used when collecting letters of endorsement. Be certain to have the original endorsements well in hand before a crisis of hours appears. Further, as was mentioned earlier, if you need a school board's approval or some agency approval, find out when they meet. You need to make a series of timelines or a master PERT Chart to plan the needed actions prior to submitting the proposal on time.

Did you have at least two or three colleagues internally review the proposal? You must. We can honestly say that when we have done that, we bat almost 1.0. When we do not, for some reason, the average drops to 0.4. Yes, internal reviewers find areas of concern or weakness. You have time to modify the proposal before it is sent out. Don't wait for the external panel to notify you of weaknesses. Or, as we like to tell our colleagues, "We don't wear our feelings on our shirtsleeves." Their feedback is critical.

In Chapter 7, it was noted that 12 or more assurances or certifications must be made, depending on the nature of the proposal. You may not have to certify against "cigarettes; and whiskey; and wild, wild people" (adapted from Spike Jones and his City Slickers). However, there will be at least nine different assurances that will be submitted when you seek federal funding. Be certain to have these items of "red tape" accomplished early. You don't want to miss a deadline because the civil rights assurance is missing.

Perhaps the title of this chapter should be "Plan, Plan, Plan." You must plan for all final activities related to the proposal.

Well, you have been diligent, planned well ahead and completed all the little detail busters previously described. The proposal is . . . *copacetic*. Now let us add just two little details. First, since you have to send 15 copies unsigned and two copies signed, and you are ready to take this stack to your official sending group, do one last check. Physically examine each proposal to count pages. Photocopying machines do make mistakes, one of the common ones being not duplicating page 12 or running page 8 twice. This is the final checkpoint. Examine each proposal to make certain that no page is missing. We have sat on NSF panels where such incidents occurred, and the proposals did not get funded because of these mistakes. How could the panel complete its review? Two pages were missing. Zero points were allocated for that section.

Second, with a significant proportion of agencies and foundations now using on-line submissions, be certain that the draft from which you are composing meets all aspects of the on-line submission format. We would encourage you to "download" those formats so you can address every detail. We have already cautioned you about "racing to the deadlines." With electronic submissions, do try to beat the deadline by a minimum of at least two or three days. "Why?" you ask. If you wait until the last hour to submit, then the servers at the agency may be overwhelmed or jammed and cause a "bottleneck." This would cause *your* proposal not to arrive on time and your efforts will be rejected. It has happened with federal agencies.

Further, if the "computer" at the agency recognizes some error or omission, you will not be able to make the necessary corrections and you will be rejected. Our plea is to plan for electronic submissions well in advance of the final hour.

One last hint: Phone the program manager to discuss possible pitfalls created by electronic submissions. Do telephone the program manager concerning the format that they want. Should it be an E-mail document or must it be a PDF file? Call especially if the guidelines do not specify the type. This will give you a "head start" on the competition.

WHY ARE PROPOSALS REJECTED?

From time to time, you will have a proposal that does not get funded. In that case, do call or write the program officer and request they send you the comments made by the review panel. Private foundations will not react to your request, but public agencies must. When you examine the panel's comments, you can then understand the "letter of declination."

Now is the time to examine the reviewer's comments. Many times your proposal has the potential for success. Resubmissions can be made only if you make the needed revisions that specifically address noted deficiencies. Let us assume that your proposal was ranked among the top, but due to budgetary restrictions you were not funded. Double-check the reviewer's comments, make any needed modifications and on the next competition resubmit. Specific aims and research strategies are the areas that often need attention and revision. Be sure to note the overall impact and innovation that your revised proposal illustrates. Revising is labor intensive, but, when funded, it is worth the effort.

Over the years, personnel in the National Science Foundation have compiled a list of weaknesses that they've observed as being common to non-funded proposals. For example, sometimes a good proposal is not funded due to a lack of funds to allocate to all meritorious proposals. The list in Model 9.1 below provides the common areas of weakness found in rejected proposals. After you check these 23 items, you should have a better understanding of the entire review process.

MODEL 9.1: Suggestions to Improve Your Proposal

Main Area	Specific or Key Points
GENERAL	
Follow Guidelines	1. Generally, the weaknesses of most proposals can be corrected by careful adherence to the guidelines.
Involve Others	2. The strongest proposals appear to be those in which the improvement plans are based on a prior assessment of institutional needs and have been carefully developed by the faculty. In these proposals, comprehensive plans and activities are set forth rather than a simple listing of needs by individual units.
NARRATIVE	
Provide Rationale	3. Provide adequate information within the narrative on the proposed plan, including evidence of a needs assessment, rationale for the proposed approach and evidence that the approach will work at the particular institution.

Main Area	Specific or Key Points
State Objectives and Activities Clearly; Tie to Budget	4. Clearly state project objectives and tie these to specific activities. Make clear the relationship between the proposed activities and the budget. Provide discussion within the narrative of all activities for which budget requests are made and include within the budget request those activities discussed in the narrative that are proposed for support.

GENERAL

Request Eligible Activities Only	5. Request support only for eligible activities and disciplines. Examples of ineligible activities are remedial courses and those based upon increased enrollment. Ineligible fields for the NSF include history, business, education, reading and clinically oriented activities. NIH proposals must show how it will aid health.
Relevant Skills of Project Director	6. Give careful thought to project personnel. This is especially true for the proposed project director, who should be selected on the basis of technical and administrative skills relevant to the project. Additionally, key project personnel must have sufficient time available to carry out project activities. Curriculum vitae should be provided for the proposed project director as well as for other key faculty and consultants.
Relevant Faculty Skills	7. Present clear evidence of existing faculty expertise in a particular strategy proposed in the project. Evidence of faculty computer experience should be presented if major computer equipment purchases have been requested in the proposal.
Timetable	8. Carefully consider the timing of activities; identify major milestones and establish a timetable for initiation and completion of these.
Describe Existing Programs	9. Describe the existing program, including faculty and facilities.
Relate to Institutional Goals	10. Indicate how the proposed plan fits into the institution's own goals or mission.
Evaluation Plan	11. Provide an adequate plan for evaluation of the project, including provision for collecting baseline data and other recordkeeping related to determining project impact.
Continuation Plan	12. Include a plan for continuation of project activities.

Main Area	Specific or Key Points
Endorsement of Central Administration	13. Be certain that the local review statement is specific and that it outlines the administration's commitment (philosophical and financial) to continuation of project activities.
Follow Guidelines	14. Stay within page limits or character limitations specified in the guide and follow format as outlined in the guide.

BUDGET

Explain Budget and Provide Justification	15. Provide a clear and detailed explanation of the proposed budget. 16. Provide justification for the proposed budget items.
List Equipment	17. List proposed equipment, materials and supplies in detail. This is especially important for equipment items costing more than $5,000. Equipment certification must be provided for special purpose equipment costing more than $10,000. Provide a list of existing major equipment holdings in areas involved in the project. Check if "buy American" is required.
Facilities & Administrative Costs (Indirect Cost Rate)	18. Provide an up-to-date F&A (indirect) cost rate for the institution. If the institution does not have an approved rate or the writer is a first-time applicant, the business officer should contact the Foundation's Division of Grants and Contracts, Policy and Cost Analysis Branch. The initial review is very time-consuming.
Role of Consultants	19. Provide information on consultants—rate of payment, extent of involvement, curriculum vitae and exact role in the project. Note that local rates are to be used and that they cannot exceed daily rate as previously noted.
Observe Limitations	20. Make sure that requests do not exceed the established maximums for dollars and duration. Requests for shorter periods of time should be proportionately reduced. Budget requests, which are out of line with stated limits, often affect the way in which reviewers react to a proposal.
Proof	21. Carefully proofread the proposal for grammatical, spelling and typographical errors. Such errors tend to give reviewers a poor impression of the proposal.
Assurances	22. Be certain that any assurances that will be required by the agency or foundation have been addressed or incorporated.
Request Comments	23. If denied, request comments and use them as a guide for resubmission.

Some of the suggestions listed in Model 9.1 address major weaknesses, while others address ways to avoid relatively minor weaknesses. It should be remembered, however, that the cumulative effect of minor problems could still result in the denial of the proposal.

THE REVIEW PROCESS

Your proposal has safely and in a timely manner found its way to the correct location for reviewing. How does that process function? Depending on the agency or foundation, it generally works like this.

The proposal is logged in and you receive a card or an E-mail message with a control number. A program officer will read the proposal and complete an evaluation form. Next, one of several techniques will be used. It may be sent to external reviewers who read and evaluate the proposal individually. The program officer tallies the reviewers' scores and, when all data are in, the proposals are rank-ordered. The top ones are funded.

A second common technique is to assemble a review panel at some city or agency. They critique each proposal individually and then discuss the merits of each collectively.

A third technique is a combination of the first two.

A fourth technique is to assemble two independent panels. Each panel is given, say, the same 10 proposals to review. Panel One is required to read and review them in order 1, 2, 3 . . . 10. Panel Two is instructed to read and review the proposals in the order 10, 9, 8 . . . 1. This method attempts to reduce panel bias and fatigue factors. Some readers start out tough and get easier as the day progresses. Other panel members are just the opposite. By having independent panels read proposals in reverse order, these two common biases tend to be cancelled.

How do you get to serve on a panel? Write a letter or send an E-mail to the specific program officer requesting that your name be added to the lists. Usually, your request will be followed by receipt of a short form that you complete and return. Being a member of a panel is a great way to learn about crafting proposals. You'll wonder why some were submitted and you'll marvel at the best-written ones. It is a must experience and it is professionally rewarding.

POST-SCRIPT

We've included another checklist that illustrates a technical review form that will help you sharpen any reasonably prepared proposal. You may be asking what could possibly be left? Chapter 10 will provide more exciting details to help you obtain those hard-to-get grant funds.

CHECKLIST: Proposal for Technical Aspects

NA = Not Applicable
U = Unsatisfactory—needs major rewriting or revising
S = Satisfactory—could use selected or minor improvement
E = Excellent—AOK as written

TECHNICAL CRITERIA

General Construction

Opening Statement	U	S	E
Lead-ins	U	S	E
Transitions between Paragraphs	U	S	E
Closing	U	S	E
"V" Development	U	S	E

Coherency

Syntax	U	S	E
Agreement (Tense or Number)	U	S	E
Logical Consistency	U	S	E
Parallel Construction	U	S	E

Clarity

Written Explicitly		U	S	E
Appropriate Word Selections		U	S	E
No Clichés		U	S	E
Terms are Defined	NA	U	S	E

Organization and Format

Side Heads Parallel Guidelines		U	S	E
Consistency of Tense		U	S	E
Correct Form for Long Quotes	NA	U	S	E
Correct Form for Short Quotes	NA	U	S	E
All Quotes Led In or Out	NA	U	S	E
Citations	NA	U	S	E
Tables	NA	U	S	E
Figures	NA	U	S	E
Spelling/Proofing		U	S	E

113

Overall Technical Evaluation	U	S	E
Qualitative Criteria			
Development of Ideas	U	S	E
Appropriate Use of Evidence	U	S	E
Data are Relevant	U	S	E
Consistent with Evaluative Criteria	U	S	E
Overall Qualitative Education	U	S	E

Chapter 10

Implementing Your Grant, Or I Have the $$, What Now?

CHAPTER SUMMARY

- Introduction
- Awards, Terms and Conditions
- Details x 2
- Getting Ready: Gathering *Your* Resources
- Behind the Scene: Financial Management
- Can't Do It Alone: Personnel Management
- The End is Near—Reporting and Project Close-out
- Post-Script

INTRODUCTION

Congratulations, you have just received notice that your proposal will be funded! Once the champagne is gone and the celebration is finished, the hardest part of completing that successful proposal begins—accomplishing what you have proposed to do! But where do you start? This chapter has six sections that will provide a road map to success.

AWARDS, TERMS AND CONDITIONS

Sponsored Project

Your proposal has been funded and is now referred to as a *sponsored project*. This term is used collectively to describe forms of external support no matter what the proposal was asking to fund. Sponsored projects are disseminated by implementing different types of awards. It is totally at the discretion of the agency which type of award mechanism will be used, although no agencies provide gifts which are free from any terms or conditions. *Please remember*, except for a few awards like fellowships or stipends, the award is given to your institution and not to you individually. You take on the role of the principal investigator or project director who is responsible overall for all aspects of the awarded project on behalf of your institution.

Were you awarded a *grant*? A grant is an award whereby money and/or direct assistance is provided to carry out approved activities of value to the recipient in order to accomplish a public purpose. If so, then simply examine the grant guidelines for any new details that must be addressed. There are always terms and conditions for spending the money. First, what is the official award date? No expenditures may be made until that date arrives. Is the award at the amount requested or has it been reduced, requiring that a new work scope and budget be prepared? Usually there is very little involvement anticipated between the agency and the recipient.

Did your award come as a *memorandum of understanding or memorandum of agreement?* A *memorandum of understanding* describes an agreed-upon common understanding between parties that reflect parallel goals, interests and lines of action, but usually does not document a particular project. A *memorandum of agreement* is similar to the memorandum of understanding, except this award type will reflect an agreed-upon project or objective that lays out the ground rules and details, with an exact dollar amount. Normally there is not that much interaction between the agency and the recipient for these award types.

Did the proposal establish a *collaborative or cooperative* agreement? A *cooperative agreement* is a legal award between a government entity (federal, state, regional, local) and the recipient to provide a service or product that benefits the general public. A *collaborative agreement* is an award between parties that contribute to a project together combining their expertise and resources for a common purpose. There is usually substantial interaction between the two parties for both of these agreements.

If your answer is "Yes" to any of the last four types, actions must be implemented as per the timeline you established in your proposal's procedures section. Details and communication during the award period are very important. The agencies that use collaborative and cooperative agreements pay extra attention to ongoing expenditures and how the project is progressing throughout the timeline.

Was your award a *contract*? A contract is a formal agreement between two parties in which the principal purpose is to acquire goods, services and/or a tangible product, which is directed by the agency's needs. Also, the principal investigator should expect more interaction with the agency. Contracts have very specific conditions, criteria and actions that must take place and in a designated manner. Now is the time to review all the above. In many cases a contract also requires a status report at prescribed times.

Was your award a *purchase order?* A purchase order is a commercial document used to request a recipient to supply a product or service in return for payment. The needed parameters (specifications, quantities, etc.) are usually provided in the purchase order to meet the awarded obligations. An example is if you were awarded an equipment grant, is there a "buy American" clause? That is, what you purchase must be made in the United States. If it is, then you need to check with your institutional fiscal and purchasing departmental representatives on how to proceed.

Was your award a *sub-award or subcontract?* What this means is another agency or entity received the initial (prime) award, but you have been designated as a subcontractor and will perform specific actions as were stated in the proposal. For example, you may have been working with a school district that received the grant, but they had involved you to perform specific activities, via subcontract. Or, your proposal may have had a subcontract with others, e.g., your institution's "Social and Economic Sciences Research Center," to conduct surveys. If yes, you need to be aware that there will be terms and conditions from both the original agency and from the entity that is issuing the sub-award or subcontract. We highly recommend that you review the terms and conditions with a contract specialist in your sponsored programs office.

Did you receive a *gift?* Typically foundations or individuals who want to support the institutional efforts for specific endeavors award gifts. The donor does not have expectations of direct economic or other tangible benefit, nor any required reporting in return for the gift. At this point contact your institution's foundation for details and be certain to send a "thank you" letter to the benefactor.

The check was in the mail: Yes, in some very rare cases, foundations or individuals will send you a check for the amount that you requested. No, you cannot simply "grab the money and run." Immediately take the check to your fiscal officer for proper establishment of an account so you may begin implementing the work plan.

DETAILS X 2

To make sure that the next few years while working on your funded project is fun and enjoyable without any unexpected glitches or misunderstandings between the agency and you, it is important for you to make sure you are familiar with all the award details. After reviewing the award, if there are any terms and conditions you have a concern about, the sponsored programs office will negotiate with the agency with the aim of coming to a happy resolution for both parties. There are two major processes that need to be reviewed very carefully before you start.

Award Acceptance

1. **The first step**, of eight, is to review the award criteria so that you have all those details outlined.

2. **Was the budget revised?** Often a budget might be revised by the awarding agency; in some cases there is a reduction in the actual amount awarded.

    For example, let us say that you requested $350,000 for a two-year project, but the amount actually awarded was only $250,000. Now the work begins, it is obvious that your scope of work must also be reduced. Caution: If you think you can do it for less than what you requested, then did you simply "pad" the budget? At this critical point immediately call a meeting of your immediate supervisor (chair or dean), the fiscal office and the sponsored programs office to plan for a reduced scope of work. When the new plan is completed, it must then be sent to the awarding agency program officer for final approval.

3. **What is the feasibility of the final award being adequate?** For example, you may have requested a specific piece of equipment that was priced at $40,000.

    The item now costs $49,000. Again, check with your fiscal office to determine if you can make any adjustments in the budget to cover this problem. In most cases a telephone call to the agency program officer can solve the issue.

4. **You now recheck your work scope.** Is there adequate funding to cover all the various activities that were originally proposed? This is usually a problem if your budget was reduced by the agency.

5. **How were the cost-sharing or -matching aspects of the project projected?**

    With many funded grants there is some required cost-sharing. Also, many foundations require some matching of funds. How did you approach this item in your proposed budget?

6. **Did the funding agency add any terms or conditions** that were not specified in the original "request for proposals" under which you submitted the proposal? It is critical to discuss these new terms with your supervisor, fiscal officer and sponsored programs office. If the terms are such that you cannot meet them, then the award might be declined. The latter is a worst-case scenario, but it has happened. In the vast majority of cases, the new terms or conditions can be easily met.

7. One last check point is offered. **Does the award meet the conditions for necessary purchase orders or other fiscal agreements?** If it does, then go on to the final action.

8. **Institutional acceptance**. At this point your authorized institutional official will accept the award as issued and sign off. This individual is usually appointed by your institution's president and is the only official that can legally bind the institution to an award. About 98 percent of the awards require sign-off by the institution. The other 2 percent are usually fellowships, stipends or earmark types of awards.

This is the moment for which you have waited! The award is official!

Budget Account Setup

Prior to establishing a budget account, it is necessary to review how the award will provide the necessary fiscal details. You do not want to be surprised in year two, as an example, to find that the budget is insufficient for whatever reason to complete your project.

Payment Schedules

There are several different types of payment schedules that agencies will use to disseminate the award funds. Some issue the full amount that will be available to your fiscal office upon notification of success. Others, like the National Science Foundation will release allocations on a yearly basis.

A common method is to pay a fixed amount on a quarterly schedule. An alternative method is quarterly, where you must submit a scope of work plan. Another payment schedule is incremental payments doled out several times over the course of each year until the full award amount has been allocated. In some rare cases, the money is awarded after completion of the project. Now, this is cause for concern because your institution must have some fiscal resources to fund your project and then await the payment. For school districts and smaller colleges this may be a major hurdle.

Line Item Conditions

On carefully double-checking the line items of the award document's budget, are there any new terms or conditions added by the agency? These are often related to equipment and personnel actions.

Allowable Costs

As you review the budget, did the agency note that some item was "non-allowable?" If so, determine how that would affect successful completion of the project. In these cases, the sponsored programs office should contact the agency program officer and negotiate a prudent resolution.

Sub-Awards

Does your proposal have any "sub-awards?" These are similar to those subcontracts that were discussed above. However, do examine these to be certain that all terms and conditions can be met.

Revenue

This is actual revenue that could be received as payment generated off of your award activities. An example would be where your award is going to support a conference and participants are charged a registration fee. That fee is considered revenue above and beyond the awarded dollars.

Guarantee Accounts

This type of account assumes authorized pre-award expenditures when, and only when, there is satisfactory assurance that there will be a formal award issued. Once the award has been received, funds are transferred from the main account to reimburse the guarantee account.

Expanded Authorities

Some federal agencies provide expanded authority to the institutions to waive prior approvals for certain award activities. One example is a first time no-cost time extension request or a revised budget that can be approved at the institutional level with notification to the agency. You need to be aware if your award could fall under this authority before starting your project.

You may be thinking to yourself, "Gee, I thought all this was done when I submitted the final draft of my proposal?" Yes, it probably was, but with the award in hand it is critical that you have the entire scope of the project in tow. You need to make sure that there is a financial expenditure plan in place based on the agency's final approved budget. And, of course, your budget office will now provide you an account on which you may begin to go to work!

The "devil in the details" has been completed. The award budget has been reviewed and accepted. The account is set up and the money is in the bank! What is next?

GETTING READY: GATHERING *YOUR* RESOURCES

It is time to take account of your resources that are available. Create a team of people who will work with you to make sure that your sponsored project is a successful experience. Each person on the team has an important role in helping you set up your project, working with you on the daily efforts and expenditures and the close-out process at the end of your award.

We recommend you identify the contacts in each of these areas that are most appropriate for your project. Invite them all to an organizational meeting to brief them on your award's project, what terms and conditions apply, what their particular roles will be during the course of the award and review the timelines/deadlines that need to be met.

Not all of these individuals will be needed for every award. As the principal investigator, you will determine what resources are required to customize the team to meet each particular award's needs.

Chair and Departmental Support give assistance for the day-to-day efforts needed to run the project smoothly. This includes any forms, requests, processes that are required with in the institution's own business areas. These also include travel arrangements, purchasing office supplies and small equipment under $3,500.

Dean and College Support as well as the chair can provide advice and guidance throughout the project's term on such topics such as policies, procedures, space considerations, staffing, commitments such as equipment match or cost-sharing and appropriate directions to take when there are issues.

Compliance Offices oversee human subjects' protection, institutional biosafety, institutional animal care and use, financial conflict of interest, environmental health and safety, radiation safety and export controls. In most institutions compliance offices are responsible for any mandatory training required for the award's key personnel.

Technology Transfer Office will help principal investigators with potential data rights, copyrights, patents and royalty activities.

Sponsored Programs Business Office is the post-award office that provides support for and oversight of post-award financial activities.

Sponsored Programs Office is the pre-award office that provides support for post-award activities that change the award's profile or terms and conditions such as time extensions, key personnel changes and revised budgets. This office can also assist in problems that arise and can serve as a liaison between the principal investigator and the agency. This office can also be a resource to help identify faculty or outside consultants whose expertise is needed for the project.

Graduate School can assist in helping identify graduate students or postdoctoral personnel that can assist in the project. This unit can also provide tuition waivers for graduate students that are supported by a sponsored project.

Human Resources will assist you with filling needed support staff, time-slip or other required positions.

Facilities and Operations works with the team for any special structural needs required to manage the project. This can include everything from remodeling to installing laboratory hoods.

Information Technology assists with any special computer or software requirements, which can include designing, programming, database creation and installations.

Purchasing Department helps with special orders such as furniture to equipment. This can include consulting and acquiring cost estimates.

Libraries will assist in ordering the needed journals, books or other similar materials for your project.

BEHIND THE SCENE: FINANCIAL MANAGEMENT

As important as the programmatic part of your award is, prudent financial management is just as important for the health of your project. You are responsible overall for making sure the funds are expended appropriately and timely throughout the entire project period. The last thing you want to happen is to come up short on funds to finish your project; or have state, federal or agency auditors standing at your office door with a binder full of questions.

As the principal investigator, you will work closely with the departmental finance person who works closely with the accountant in the sponsored programs business office. These are very important people that promote proper financial stewardship by managing the invoicing and billing, accounts receivable and cash management. The sponsored programs business office also prepares and submits the required financial status reports, certifies time and effort plus program revenue. They act as a resource for the principal investigator on proper direct cost-sharing and budget practices. One of their responsibilities, as well as the principal investigator, is to be very familiar with OMB Circulars.

All awards are subject to regulations. Failure to comply can result in audit findings, disallowance of cost, federal funding being cut off to your institution; fines, penalties and even, in certain circumstances, jail time. The policies and procedures of your institution, college or department are included in these regulations, and you need to become very familiar with them. For non-federal funds you need to see your award documents for specifics.

Not all regulations apply to all awards, so you need to become familiar with the appropriate regulations that will apply to your funds. We have already discussed agency terms and conditions that are directly accountable to the agency. The main regulations that are applicable to federal funds are:

- OMB Circular A-21 (cost principles for educational institutions)
- OMB Circular A-110 (uniform administrative requirements for federal grants and agreements)

- OMB Circular A-133 (audits of states, local governments and non-profits)
- CAS (Cost Accounting Standards)
- FAR (Federal Acquisition Regulations for federal contracts)
- F&A (Facilities and Administrative cost rate agreement)

We realize that this is not exciting reading. However, becoming familiar with the regulations that are applicable to your award can save you much grief later if there are audit findings. As the principal investigator, work with your department finance person at the beginning of your award's budget period to develop an overall plan for the commitment of the funds to meet the required regulations. We highly recommend that you approve all expenditures to be charged against your award; review the budget statements and expenditures on a regular basis; and meet every couple of months to sit down with your department of finance person to review your budget status.

Other finance management issues to be monitored are effort certifications, cost-sharing requirements (if required), cost transfers and cost rebudgeting. When you take on the role of principal investigator, this includes assuming accountability for deficits, uncollectables and other disallowances that might occur under the award account. Your department finance person working with you should watch for overdrafts and minimize expenditure transfer requests.

The other person that is very important for your financial award health is your sponsored programs business office accountant that monitors your accounts for activity requiring actions. In addition, this individual will provide: the general university-level fiscal administration; interpretation of regulations, terms and conditions; monthly budget statements to department finance person and you; and all financial reports.

With your human resource team member make sure that you verify your institution's compensation policies. Normally soft funded personnel are not paid any different rate than those that are not on an award. You do not want to make promises on salaries on which you won't be able to follow through.

A tip to help you with the financial management is to develop a financial shadow bookkeeping system. Since you need to monitor the expenditures and you can't delegate 100 percent this responsibility to the accountants, your records will give you a more "real-time" idea and justification on where the expenses are and what is the budget's bottom line.

Another tip is to not overspend in one area. Again, keep in good communication with your departmental financial person. You will probably at some point need to rebudget some of your budget line items to make sure there is a continuous balance between your budgeted amounts and your actual expenditures.

Another tip is to plan for an audit. As we stated earlier in this section, continually monitor your expenditures and be knowledgeable of the allowable and non-allowable costs for your award. If you are uncertain about an allowable expense, contact your funding agency's program manager.

The last tip is to not hire your spouse or other relatives to work on your project. Do not create expenditures with a company, vendor or entity that your spouse owns or you serve in an official capacity with. The last thing you want to do is give the appearance that there is a conflict of interest that is influencing where the funding is being spent. If you feel that there is something wrong with this type of activity, there probably is. Do not take the risk doing it! It is all about how you are perceived!

YOU CAN'T DO IT ALONE: PERSONNEL MANAGEMENT

Obviously when you were preparing your proposal budget and thinking through your objectives, there was consideration given to what type and how many personnel you will need to manage the project's work. Defining the roles of your personnel and the sequential process of hiring and supervising is so important in meeting your project's goals.

Your department or college's personnel/office manager should be part of your team. Once they understand what you need for each position, they will work with your human resource team member to pull together the appropriate type of position descriptions. They will assist you with completing forms and proceeding through your institution's hiring process. Be sure that you are kept in the loop through this process, as your input on who or what expertise you need will be invaluable to you later on down the road. Annual performance reviews are very important for those working on a project. They are used to not only evaluate the person's performance, but the performance itself can be used as a benchmark indicating what progress is being made on the project.

Have the graduate school team member help you identify graduate students that would work well on your project. Many institutions will offer tuition waivers and other perks for those graduate students that are supported on soft money.

Continuous training and education is sometimes mandatory and always crucial to keeping your personnel updated on the project's progress, or maybe updates from the funding agency, or sharing your progress and financial reports. The better an employee is kept informed and part of the team, the better quality your project will be from the inside out!

THE END IS NEAR—REPORTING AND PROJECT CLOSE-OUT

Congratulations! You can just about see the end of your project! But first, at the absolute minimum 30 days out from the award termination date, you need to decide if a time extension is needed, or whether submitting a renewal proposal to continue the project for another award period is desired. If either of these scenarios is planned, you need to work with your team to start these processes as mentioned earlier in the book.

If you determine to proceed ahead with the close-out, then it is time to refresh your memory on the award's terms and conditions concerning what needs to be done for closing out the project. If you need verification concerning the award's close-out terms, then contact your agency's program manager. Also, consult with your department and college team members on any requirements they might have for the close-out process. How many different team members will be involved in this process? When are the different reports due—30, 60 or 90 days after the termination of the award? Pay special attention to the timeline. Make sure that your colleagues have sufficient time to do their part and either return the information to you or submit it to the agency on time. We suggest you make a "to do" list parallel with the timeline while reviewing the award document and briefing the team. Below are the areas you usually need to start working with to begin this process.

Tidying up

Review of final agency, institutional, department requirements (project team)—A team meeting at the beginning of this process is advised to do a full review of the requirements.

Closing Accounts (department finance officer)—You should work with the department finance person to make a plan for expending the remaining funds before the termination date. At this point in time, avoid making high-risk transactions if at possible.

Final Financial OMB A-133 Audit (sponsored programs business office)—The team member from this office will do a final review of expenditures and remaining allocations based on the OMB Circular. If necessary, they will invoice the agency for remaining outstanding funds.

Invention or Technology Transfer (sponsored programs business office)—The team member from this area will obtain any invention information from you, and the intellectual property office.

Final Reports

As the investigator, you are totally responsible for making sure the final reports are submitted. The financial and invention reports are generated from the sponsored programs business office. You will need to work with the team members from this area to make sure they are completed and submitted separately from the other reports.

125

The final technical reports are so important, not only to the funding agency but also to you! Getting your report in on time (remember to pay attention to the timeline) reflects to the agency that you are efficient, competent, detail-oriented and successful. You don't want the agency to keep nagging you about an overdue report, or having attention drawn to yourself, with the authorized institutional official knocking on your office door telling you to get the report submitted! In the worst-case scenario, the agency might request that all funds be returned, or that they cut off any further funding to your institution until the report has been submitted and accepted.

Be sure to provide all the information that is requested. There are reasons why they are asking certain questions. You don't want to leave any sections or boxes empty. Also, be sure that all the financial data are complete. This information is very important in demonstrating your accomplishments.

Most importantly the technical report needs to reflect that you did what you said you were going to do! We suggest in the narrative section of the report that you first list each of your objectives that were presented in the proposal, and then follow that with the project's outcomes. This format will clearly reflect that you remained focused and committed to the work that was proposed and funded by the agency.

Many principal investigators are nervous about including in the report failures or efforts that did not turn out as expected. Failures and unexpected outcomes are as informative as those that are just what you were hoping for. Be matter-of-fact about these outcomes, explaining what happened, why and what you learned from them.

Another possible reason for not accomplishing what you said you would do is factors that were beyond your control. For example, not being able to find the right personnel, or not being able to get access to materials, libraries, certain publications that you needed. In the last few years we have had principal investigators that weren't able to move forward on their projects because of current downsized economy and political issues between the United States and other countries. This type of information also needs to be included in your final report. Remember that the agency has the right to decline the report if not satisfied with the results, or feels the report is incomplete. If information is not accurately reported, there certainly is the implication for fraud.

Below are the standard reports that are requested at the termination of an award. Some agencies will require more reports, some less. Almost every agency has a different preferred format. Some formats are very informal, while others are very structured, with boxes and fields that need to be completed. Most federal agencies require electronic reports. There are still quite a few non-federal agencies that require hard copy.

Technical or Final Project (principal investigator)—The reports *must* be complete and accurate. You do not want misconduct in science issues.

Financial (sponsored programs business office)—The team member from this office will prepare the final financial reports and submit them to the agency. They will close the account once all reports have been submitted and accepted.

Publications (principal investigator)—In order for them to be reproduced, they must reflect consistent and validated results.

Invention (sponsored programs business office)—The team member from this office will prepare a report that is submitted to the agency, indicating any possible outcomes of technology or products that would generate future revenue.

No matter what the final reports look like, all agencies will require some type of report. David Bauer, a well-known presenter on proposal writing, developed the "Swiss cheese" concept that can be used to help you during the award period to be prepared for the final report. At the first, when your team and you are reviewing the terms and conditions for the final report, create folders for each of the different requirements. During the course of working on your project, you will just drop in the folders information that will be needed when you are ready to start writing the final report. This would include any progress or quarterly reports you prepare, budget statements, any award changes or exceptions made, etc. during the life of the award. This way, you will not be sitting at your computer wondering what happened in year two that affected one of your objectives. You will be able to pull out the appropriate folder and find the documentation.

POST-SCRIPT

What could possibly be left? Good luck and much $uccess in your proposal efforts. And don't forget to send a note of thanks to the program officer when you receive that letter that begins, "We are pleased . . ."

A Model of a Funded Proposal

Appendix A is a copy of a funded proposal. The names of individuals are changed, as are the locales. Everything else is verbatim and the model follows the guidelines exactly.

The budget that follows has been deliberately left "open-ended." In that manner, you can fill in data and gain practice. If the data were given, you would not actively participate. To save space, two-page vitae of the personnel are excluded, as are the letters of endorsement and various assurances. However, the vitae follow the previously presented model.

The 11 side heads in the proposal are quoted directly from the guidelines.

NORTH STATE RURAL SCIENCE PROJECT

1. Proposal Summary

This project is designed to meet the expressed science education needs of the K-12 state science teachers in the North Service Area. These needs have been documented to be a top priority and confirmed by the September 1993 North Science Conference and 1994 intensive review and critique. The goal is to develop science teachers who will provide district leadership for systemic changes in science curriculum and instructional strategies.

The objectives of the project are to: (1) provide selected science teachers with an understanding of the constructivist model of teaching science; (2) model an integrated science, technology and societal program for teachers to use in their classrooms; (3) establish a support network of constructivist-oriented science teachers who model constructivist principles; and (4) implement strategies that encourage minorities, especially Native Americans, Hispanics and women, to continue the study of science.

A one-week, intensive workshop will be held in Redding for selected science and technology teachers where participants develop and prepare constructivist lessons for their students.

2. State Priority Addressed

The state priorities are those of: (1) developing competency for teachers in the use of instructional technology within the areas of science and mathematics at the middle level, (2) developing competency in mathematics and science for teachers assigned to teach these subjects at the secondary level and (3) developing strategies for improving the access to instruction for historically underserved populations.

3. Program Audience and Development

This project is the product of a planning and writing team from (1) representative teachers of the area, (2) staff of the selected school districts and (3) North State University faculty. At NSU, the Science Improvement Center (SIC) initially conducted an extensive needs assessment during the 1993–4 school year. The assessment indicated a need for additional training at the middle and secondary levels to augment the training delivered by NSU the last two years at the elementary level. Participants indicated a need to: (1) develop a constructivist approach in teaching at all levels for all children, (2) integrative up-to-date instructional technology into the pedagogy and (3) establish a regional network for the rural schools for a support base.

A broad-based advisory team representing the area was formed to develop this project. Team members included Bill Jackson, Superintendent of Paradise Schools; Jane Perez; Assistant Superintendent Redding Schools; Fred Daniels, Superintendent of Red Bluff Schools; and Cedric Brown, Superintendent of Willows Schools.

Teachers who participated were Ray Fitzpatrick, Colusa; Victor Peterson, Red Bluff; Vicky Kingsley, Willows; Sam Johnson, Yuba City; Lance Rodgers, Live Oak; Mike Wilson, Upper Lake; and Patty Renz, Redding. They collaborated with the team led by Harvey Chandler, Director of SIC, and Charles Judd, Professor of Science Instruction from NSU. This proposal was jointly written by the above persons. Private schoolteachers will be invited to the workshop and they have a history of high participation in NSU projects.

This project addresses both the needs of the underrepresented minorities (i.e., women, Hispanic and Native American) and regular students. Hispanics constitute a growing population in school districts in this area and Native American children are also widely distributed. The minority population is rapidly expanding in most districts.

Middle and secondary science teachers provide the leadership in science to rural school districts that have few resource or support specialists. Many times the teacher serves science needs through a wide grade level range. Therefore, it is essential that these teachers have an opportunity to practice instructional strategies necessary for systemic change in the science curriculum in their districts.

Between 1991 and 1995, NASA grants to NSU have supported training for elementary teachers to become resources for their staffs in this geographical area. They do, however, look to the science content specialist for help and guidance. This proposal builds a leadership cadre of middle and secondary science teachers.

4. Program Goals

The primary goal of this project is to develop a leadership cadre of middle and secondary science teachers with an understanding of the constructivist model of teaching science.

The second goal is to infuse strategies to enhance science teaching with women and minorities as part of this project.

These goals will be accomplished by the following objectives.

(1) *Selected science topics will be explored with teachers in physical, biological and earth sciences.*

Laboratory activities will be organized relating to concepts of water quality, geology, environmental science and health. The concepts associated with water quality will be carefully selected to expand each teacher's background for *the* appropriate sciences being taught in the respective grade levels. All participants will be provided with common experiences in conducting water quality studies in the area. Thus, the content will be relevant to each participant in his or her respective program.

(2) *Selected topics that parallel objective one will be organized as a model for participants to integrate appropriate technology with mathematics, technology and societal issues that relate to the theme of water quality.*

Materials will be provided so that teachers may observe models of curriculum integration. The use of technology will be illustrated as a platform by which technology becomes an integral part of planning and teaching. The Science–Technology–Society (STS) model will be exemplified through a common water quality experience.

(3) *Illustrative science materials for women, Hispanic and Native American pupils will be featured.*

Specific sets of materials will be provided so that the teachers can construct specific lessons that can be integrated into each teacher's science program.

(4) *Peer support groups will be established to provide coaching on "process" skills, e.g., thinking skills, questioning techniques, small-group work and program evaluation.*

Small groups of participants will be organized into support teams by school so that the interactive processes so essential to teaching constructivist-oriented science may take place.

During the workshop experiences will be provided and modeled for guided inductive and unguided inductive inquiry by using water quality research as the common theme. These two elements form the bases for the programs being reviewed as exemplars and are components of constructivist science teaching.

The above goals and objectives relate directly to the state priorities of providing greater access to science for underrepresented and underserved students. Minority teachers will be personally invited to attend the workshop by designated school district liaisons.

The above illustrates a model that utilizes local resource persons and builds a cadre network of teachers who are in close proximity.

Significance. This project has great significance in that it is the first time that a model created in one Eisenhower project is being disseminated and field-tested in a different context and geographic setting. This in-service mechanism uses intensive training with some follow-up activities that helps to keep the network established.

The theoretical basis and original model are described at the end of the next section that is titled "Research Basis."

5. Program Activities

Workshop. A one-week, two-phase workshop will be conducted in June 1995, following school dismissal. The tentative dates are June 26–30, 1995. Ten specific points will be incorporated into the workshop design.

1. Integrated Concepts and Processes
2. Teacher Materials
3. Student Materials
4. Constructivist Model
5. National Standards/America and Goals 2000
6. Instructional Strategies
7. Evaluation
8. Special Needs
9. Electronic Networking, e.g., Email, Electronic Bulletin Boards
10. Cooperative Research Teams

During all sessions, the participants will always be involved with direct experiences with science materials needed to determine water quality—the theme being used as an exemplar. Integrated in the instruction will be instructing minority and disabled pupils so that science can be taught meaningfully to them.

The evening format (Monday through Thursday) will be from 7:00 p.m. to 9:00 p.m. Three distinct aspects will be:

1. Cooperative research teams to share data
2. Development of pilot models for use "back home"
3. Networking among the selected schools

Water sampling sites will be selected along rivers, e.g., Mill and Stony, and from local area ponds. During 1995–6, students will also test deep well samples. As data are collected, students will use mathematics and statistical analyses to compile a longitudinal record of activities. These data will be released to local media on a bi-monthly basis.

We will also use teacher resource persons to help with the academic year in-service component. This will entail providing instruction to other teachers who were unable to attend the summer phase. Tentatively, they are Lance Rodger, Live Oak and Betty McDonald, Colusa.

At least two follow-up, problem-solving meetings are planned for academic year 1995–6. Follow-up session number one will be held in conjunction with the annual regional science conference, to be held in Chico, November 3–4, 1995. Follow-up session number two will be held in Redding. During these sessions, we will meet to discuss the implementation of the project. During the fall conference, we will also present an orientation about the program for others.

Table A.1 shows the program's activities.

Research Basis. Lev Vygotsky (1962) appears to be the founder of the constructivist philosophy of teaching and learning. This model requires a strong interaction between the presented material and the learner's personal thought processes and interactions. A major conclusion of Anne Batey and Sylvia Hart-Landsberg (1993) was that rural science teachers strongly endorsed the use of multiple senses that created an emotional engagement by which to create contextual memories. The latter implies that, in an intensive workshop, teachers will "learn" more and that they have high probability of teaching as they were taught.

Again, the Batey and Hart-Landsberg classic, *Riding the Wind*, emphasizes the importance of direct access to materials to stimulate science aptitudes. Their report is most relevant as all participants in the project were from rural schools of the area.

Howard Gardner's (1983) seven forms of human intelligence shows that activities must facilitate the solving of problems or the creation of specific products. Thus, teachers and students need to be given opportunities to think in different ways. This project does that with the broad array of activities, built-in personal exchanges and multi-methodologies.

P. Cobb, E. Yackel and T. Wood (1992) also noted that effective constructivist learning models require that students be encouraged to ask questions. Therefore, it is critically important that teachers do not use questioning as a way to belittle students. D. C. Orlich et al. (1994) provided a tested model that shows how teachers can use questioning, small-group discussions and inquiry in a most humane manner and yet meet the conditions of constructivist learning.

In addition, this general model has had one successful pilot project in the state. Twenty teachers in the Lassen Educational Service District evaluated this model in 1994 as being most usable and relevant to science teaching and meeting the state's Science Framework.

References

Batey, Anne and S. Hart-Landsberg (1993). *Riding the Wind*. Portland: Northwest Regional Educational Laboratory. A final report, "Rural Leadership in Science Mathematics Education."

TABLE A.1 Immersion model schedule

	Monday	Tuesday	Wednesday	Thursday	Friday
8 a.m. to noon	Project Start-up Define Problem Form Research Groups Water Quality Data Gathering	Data Collecting of Water Quality on Site	Water Shed Management Data Gathering on Site	Develop Curricular Model for Districts Use of Technology Input Data into Regional Data Bank	Critique of Curriculum Models Integration of Technology
noon to 1 p.m.			—— LUNCH ——		
1 p.m. to 5 p.m.	Work with Cadre to Determine Water Characteristics on Site Preparing of Data Reports by Research Teams	Analyzing Data Laboratory	Modeling of Constructivist Principles Women and Minorities Workshop	Curriculum Development Essentials for Gifted Students	Evaluation Models Plans for 1995–6 AY Completion
5 p.m. to 7 p.m.			—— DINNER ——		
7 p.m. to 9 p.m.	U.S. Army Corps of Engineers	Teachers Working with Actual Research Teams	"SITE" Network Design	Network Building Use of Technology	

Cobb, P., E. Yackel and T. Wood (1992). "A Constructivist Alternative to the Representational View of Mind in Mathematics Education." *Journal for Research in Mathematics Education*, 23(1): 2–33.

Gardner, H. (1983). *Frames of Mind: The Theory of Multiple Intelligences.* New York: Basic Books.

Orlich, D. C., et al. (1994). *Teaching Strategies: A Guide to Better Instruction,* 4th ed. Lexington, MA: D.C. Heath.

Vygotsky, L. (1962). *Thought and Language.* Cambridge, MA: M.I.T. Press.

6. Program Personnel

Below is a listing of personnel, their duties and responsibilities in this project.

1. *Harvey Chandler, Project Co-Director.* Chandler is the Director of the Science Improvement Center at NSU. He has developed and demonstrated STS projects working with different cultures in the state and internationally. He will: (1) aid in planning, organizing and coordinating the project; (2) be responsible for fiscal commitments through NSU's business offices; (3) be liaison with the school districts; (4) assist in teaching the STS model; (5) conduct follow-up activities during first quarter 1995–6 academic year; and (6) prepare the final report.

2. *David Lawrence, Project Co-Director.* Lawrence is an associate professor at NSU. He is the President of the state science teachers' association and is very active in teacher education. He is a geologist and has been involved in numerous teacher workshops using the constructivist model. He will: (1) coordinate and illustrate teaching geology in an interactive model using water quality as the common theme; (2) assist in curriculum design; and (3) help with safety instruction.

3. *Charles Judd, Professor of Science Instruction at NSU.* He will: (1) evaluate the workshop and follow-up activities; (2) provide models illustrating constructivist, inquiry and assessment techniques; and (3) help prepare the final report.

4. *Lance Rodgers, Science Department Chair, Live Oak High School.* He has a B.S. and M.S. in geology and industrial experience in hydrology. He will serve as a water chemistry resource person and also follow-up as noted in the proposal.

5. *N. D. Sanchez, Supervisor of Instructional Technology at the LESD* [Lassen Educational School District]. He has taught science in the public schools for over 30 years. He will supervise and instruct the appropriate use of instructional technology in an integrated STS program.

6. *Christine Jones, Project Assistant.* She has had extensive experience assisting the conduct of science education projects at NSU since 1989. She will be responsible for secretarial/technical assistance to the project throughout the funding period.

7. *Bart Hixon, Science Supervisor, Lassen Educational School District, Susanville.* He will coordinate the dissemination of the LESD project with North teachers.

8. *Betty McDonald, Native American Science Teacher, Colusa School District.* She will provide instruction in teaching science to minority students and will be a resource specialist as noted in the proposal.

7. Other Program Resources

The project co-directors will secure all necessary buildings and facilities. The site scheduled for this project is Redding, as it is central to the area.

The Redding School District will provide all necessary buildings and laboratory facilities. The study site scheduled for this project is the Redding geographic area, as it has adequate housing and is adjacent to many potential test sites.

NSU will provide, at no cost to the project, all of the "large" water quality test kits for laboratory analysis. Each "research team" will perform its own testing, and during the follow-up years each teacher will have an opportunity to utilize test kits at his/her own school at no cost. Federal agencies, e.g., the U.S. Army Corps of Engineers and Fish and Wildlife Service, have offered their resources.

The Lassen Peak Consortium has endorsed the linking of rural teachers into a sharing network.

Area private schoolteachers have a history of participating in state and federally funded staff development programs in science with the rural schools. Science teachers in these schools will be invited to participate.

8. Program Administration

As was noted in Section Six, the project has two co-directors. Harvey Chandler will direct major project activities. All administrative activities have been divided so that supervision, monitoring and evaluation are distributed in a logical manner. Chandler will coordinate budgetary aspects of the project emanating from NSU. David Lawrence will coordinate all personnel who participate in the project and will work closely with Chandler in the administration of the project. Each has had significant experience in conducting and directing science education projects.

N. D. Sanchez will coordinate all technology aspects (computer networking) of the proposed project.

9. Institutional Capacity

North State University has identified science education as a top priority. This is reflected by the efforts in working to enhance elementary science education. However, the needs assessment and focus group of October 1994 strongly supported an extension of services to the middle and high school levels. Secondary teachers (and administrators) strongly supported the dissemination of the successful 1994 LESD model into this project to encompass middle and secondary teachers. The NSU group has the resources of its institution to be marshaled to help this project be successful.

North State University is known nationally for its science education efforts. Harvey Chandler is the Director of the *institutionally supported* Science Improvement Center. He is an immediate past president of the state science teachers' association and has had multicultural experience in the Philippines, Japan, Malaysia and Thailand. Chandler has co-directed three very successful school district projects in science education between 1988 and 1994.

135

David Lawrence is known nationally for his research in geology and reform efforts in science education, K-16. He has been an award-winning teacher at both the state and national levels. He is currently president of the state science teachers association. He has co-directed several science education projects.

Charles Judd is very active in science education and has had extensive experience working with science teachers in rural areas and serves on two national boards for curriculum projects. He was a coordinator for the innovative and federally funded "Project Smart," which focused on very rural science teachers from 1991–3. Judd has published on science evaluation and has evaluated science projects since 1971.

10. Program Evaluation

The project evaluation has three components.

1. *Workshop Evaluation*. Several evaluative instruments will be used to measure participant reactions to the summer training phases. Our model is designed to provide feedback to the project staff. Content evaluations and process evaluations will be administered to allow for immediate adjustments. This procedure has been used successfully and a longitudinal study by Judd showed the model to be highly stable — even over a 21-year period.
2. *Teachers' Instruction.* The second component will be to establish a baseline on science teaching strategies. Teachers will be asked to complete baseline data. Specific information will include:

   a. Amount of time teaching science
   b. Questioning strategies used
   c. Inquiry techniques used (constructivist model)
   d. Student time-on-task for science
   e. Teacher and student talk during science periods

   During the spring of 1996, Judd will seek the above information and compare findings with the baseline data and prepare a report for the State Eisenhower Program Officer (SEPO).
3. *Pupil Evaluations*. Pupil science attitudes scales will be prepared to determine the affective dimensions of the project on students. An instrument will be constructed under the direction of Judd and administered in fall of 1995 and spring 1996. Data will be shared with SEPO.

11. Program Continuation

As the science and training model is field-tested, it will become an important factor in the K-12 science, mathematics and technology programs for the area schools. This project could have a major impact on the direction that science education will take at NSU. This will be the model to take school districts into the 21st Century and help meet the Goals of America 2000!

The establishment of a formal network of educators will ensure continued sharing and developing of ideas.

INSTITUTION				PROJECT DIRECTOR		
North State University				Harvey Chandler		
TITLE OF PROJECT				**FINANCIAL/BUDGET OFFICE CONTACT**		
North State Rural Science Project				Office of Grant & Research Development		
					OTHER FUNDS	PROPOSED EISENHOWER GRANT ($)
1. PERSONNEL		Eisenhower Funded Mos.				
Key Personnel Salaries (Faculty Administration)	Acad.	Sum.	Cal.			
A. Salaries I. H. Chandler		.5				
II. D. Lawrence		.5				
III. C. Judd		.23				
IV.						
B. Fringe Benefits (26%) # Benefits @ 9%						
Support Personnel (Clerical, Grad, Assistants)						
A. Salaries I. Tech. Asst. II, 155 hrs. @ $16/hr						2,480
II.						
III.						
IV.						
B. Fringe Benefits (16%)						
TOTAL PERSONNEL COSTS						
2. PARTICIPANT COSTS						
A. Tuition						
B. Fees						
C. Books						
D. Materials						
E. Travel						3,000
F. Room and Board						5,808
G. Other: Stipend $125 x 25 = $3,125; 100 x 25 x 2 = $5,000						8,125
TOTAL PARTICIPANT COSTS						16,933
3. OTHER TRAVEL						
A. Mileage (Institute and Site Visits)						280
B. State Per Diem						1,254
4. SUPPLIES						
A. Kit Materials, Demo Project Supplies, Phone, Mailing						2,000
B.						
5. EQUIPMENT RENTAL						
A. Four telephone lines in Redding for computer linkage						500
B.						
6. CONTRACTUAL						
A. Hixon, McDonald, Sanchez						3,141
B. Teachers—Two Teachers						1,098
7. OTHER						
A.						
B.						
C.						
8.						
TOTAL DIRECT COSTS (Sum of Items 1–7)						
9.						
INDIRECT COSTS (@ 8%) (Sum of Item 8)						
10.						
TOTAL COSTS (Sum of Items 8 & 9)						

FIGURE A.1 Eisenhower budget summary

137

EISENHOWER BUDGET SUMMARY

NORTH STATE
RURAL SCIENCE PROJECT

Budget Narrative Detail

1. Personnel

    All NSU personnel are paid as per established salary.

Key Personnel Salaries (Faculty, Administration)

1.	H. Chandler	.5 month @ $_____/mo	$_____
2.	D. Lawrence	.5 month @ $_____/mo	$_____
3.	C. Judd	.23 month @ $_____/mo	$_____

A. **Fringe Benefits**

    26% for #1 and #2 $_____   9% for #3 $_____ $_____

Support Personnel Salaries

A.	Tech. Asst. II; 155 hrs. @ $16 per hour	$2,480
B.	Fringe Benefits (16%)	$_____

TOTAL PERSONNEL COSTS $_____

2. Participant Costs

E. Travel (Mileage)

SUMMER INSTITUTE: Each participant will receive an average of $40
25 participants x $40

                                                                    $1,000

FALL AND SPRING FOLLOW-UPS: Each participant will receive
an average of $40
25 participants x $40 (fall and spring, $40 each time) $2,000

F. Room and Board

SUMMER INSTITUTE: 22 participants will receive lodging and means at
$66 per diem
$66 per diem x 22 participants x 4 nights $5,808

G. Other (Stipends)

SUMMER INSTITUTE: $125 per participant
$125 x 25 participants $3,125

FALL AND SPRING FOLLOW-UPS: $100 per participant
$100 x 25 participants x 2 follow-ups $5,000
        TOTAL PARTICIPANTS COSTS $16,933

3.   Other Travel

A.   Mileage

SUMMER INSTITUTE:
Chandler and Judd from Sonoma/Chico
One round trip (288 pt. to pt.; 22 vicinity)
250 miles @ .28/mile $70

Lawrence from Sonoma/Chico
One round trip (228 pt. to pt.; 22 vicinity)
250 miles @ .28/mile $70

SITE VISITS AND FOLLOW-UP
2 days total—Chandler and Judd
Mileage: $70/each trip $140

B.   Lodging

SUMMER INSTITUTE
$66/day for Chandler (5), Lawrence (5), Judd (5)
$66 x 5 = $330 x 3 $990

SITE VISITS AND FOLLOW-UP
Site visits plus spring follow-up, Redding
Chandler (2), Judd (2)
Per Diem $66 x 2 days x 2 $264
        TOTAL OTHER TRAVEL COSTS $1,534

4.   Supplies
Included are expendable costs and materials for teachers to "take home"
for demonstration purposes, long distance telephone, faxing, mail
services, reproduction of joint material, and project supplies and kits
for teachers.
        TOTAL SUPPLIES $2,000

5.   Equipment Rental
Four telephone lines in Redding for computer linkage $500
        TOTAL EQUIPMENT RENTAL $500

6. Contractual (Consultants)

Bart Hixon	2 days @ $250/day	$500
Mileage	392 miles @ $0.25/mi	$98
Per Diem	2 days x $66	$132
N. D. Sanchez	4 days @ $250/day	$1,000
Mileage	350 miles @ $0.28/mi	$98
Per Diem	4 days x $66	$264
Betty McDonald	2 days @ $250	$500
Teacher Follow-Up	3 days @ $150	$450
Travel Average	$25 x 3 days	$75
Meal Allowance	$8 x 3 days	$24
Two Teachers		
Follow-Up for 3 days		
Stipend	$150/day x 2 x 3 days	$900
Travel	Average $25 x 2 x 3 days	$150
Meal Allowance	$8 x 2 x 3 days	$48
TOTAL CONSULTANT COSTS	$4,239	

7. Other (N/A)

8. Total Direct Costs (Sum of Items 1–7)

9. Indirect Costs (@ 8%) (Sum of Item 8)

10. Total Costs (Sum of Items 8 & 9)

NOTE: Indirect cost rate is fixed at 8 percent.

Appendix B

A Basic "Toolbox" for Grant-Seekers

To aid in your successful search for funding sources, we have provided a basic "toolbox." It provides important information about agencies or foundations that may yield financial assistance to your proposals. Included is a selection of Internet websites. Collectively, these will help make your search more efficacious. All entries were actuated at the time of publication, however a word of caution: web addresses are subject to change or deletion without notice. Most of the tools connected with federal agencies are free to access, while the tools for non-governmental agencies are accessed on a subscription or purchase base.

BASIC TOOLS TO CONNECT WITH THE FEDS

Catalog of Federal Domestic Assistance (CFDA). The CFDA contains descriptions of all federal programs, including information on authorizing legislation, purposes, eligibility, appropriations, information contacts, application and award processes and related programs. The CFDA assigns numbers to each program (an absolute must-have tool). The 2,611-page CFDA is online at: www.cfda.gov.

Code of Federal Regulations (CFR). An accompanying item to the FR, this codifies all permanent rules published in the FR. The document is online at: www.gpoaccess.gov/cfr.

Department of Education (DOED). This website (www.ed.gov) forecasts funding opportunities under the Department of Education that includes the discretionary grant programs. The site is organized into eight principal areas. Included in the document are deadline dates, contact persons, available funds, estimated average size of awards and number of awards; all programs are listed under the CFDA No. 84. This alone is a great tool for busy educators, who can then anticipate and plan for more systematic grant proposal submissions.

Department of Energy (DOE). DOE supports competitive proposals that address energy, environmental and nuclear challenges and needs of the United States. http://energy.gov.

Environmental Protection Agency (EPA). EPA is the federal agency that is responsible for protecting the environment and people's health both nationally and internationally. It supports hundreds of awards each year from basic research, to exchanges, to leadership programs associated with the environment. http://epa.gov.

FedBizOpps (formerly Commerce Business Daily). FedBizOpps releases virtually all federal government requests for bids, services and buildings. This is really a device for "professionals." Amateurs can't compete. Over 34,000 active federal-funding opportunities are listed online at: www.fbo.gov and also at: http://cbdnet.gpo.gov.

Federal Register (FR). The FR contains program regulations (proposed and final), announcements of deadlines and funding criteria. This is a must for the individual, group or institution desirous of seeking federal funds. Access online at: www.gpoaccess.gov/fr/index.html.

GRANTS.GOV. This is a compendium of federal grants. This resource is a central storehouse for information on over 1,000 grant programs and provides access to approximately $500 billion in annual awards. Detailed information, program highlights and various milestones are provided. Accessible online at http://grants.gov/applicants/find_grant_opportunities.jsp.

Federal Agencies

All federal agencies can be accessed by simply going online to a search engine like Google, Yahoo! or Bing and entering the agency name. There are many federal agencies that support basic and applied research, programmatic and project competitive programs. Below are some of the more utilized federal websites.

National Endowment for the Arts (NEA) and the National Endowment for the Humanities (NEH). Both of these endowments were created by the National Foundation on the Arts and Humanities Act of 1965 in support of public and preservation programs through education and research nationally and through 56 humanities and art councils. www.nea.gov and www.neh.gov.

National Institutes of Health (NIH). NIH is made up of 27 different institutes and centers, each with its own specific research specialty. This federal agency is tasked to reduce or eliminate illness and disability through promoting health and knowledge of living systems. www.nih.gov.

National Science Foundation (NSF). A major federal agency that provides many millions of dollars for research, development and in-service training is the NSF. At this site you can locate just about everything you ever wanted to know about programs, grants, awards and pending news. The NSF covers everything from the hard sciences, like engineering and biological research, to social sciences and education. www.nsf.gov.

U.S. Department of Agriculture (USDA). USDA supports basic and applied research and projects that entail all aspects of farming, agriculture and food that meet the needs of those involved in activities both nationally and internationally. http://usda.gov.

USA.gov for Nonprofits. This is the official information and services from the U.S. government. It provides a virtual library of resources for federal grant-seekers. This free online service may be accessed at: www.usa.gov/Business/Nonprofit.shtml.

CONNECTING WITH NON-GOVERNMENTAL SOURCES

Large Tools to Tap Private Foundations

This is by no means the ultimate listing of resources to help you find potential funding opportunities. These are directories, websites and search engines that are some of the most used to find funding sources.

Annual Register of Grant Support: A Directory of Funding Sources (the *Register*). The *Register* provides information on over 3,000 North American grant-making groups. Included are foundations, businesses, unions, governmental agencies, professional associations and others. This is an excellent first source to initiate contact with potential funders. http://books.infotoday.com/directories/anreg.shtml

Directory of Grants in the Humanities. This directory lists 3,635 funding potentials for the humanities nationally and internationally. www.grantselect.com/pubs.humanities.

Educational Grants Alert is a free online service that focuses on K-12 education grants. Various private and government funding opportunities are identified. This is a helpful resource with timely tips. For more information, contact jmizereck@grantsalert.com.

Foundation Center. As a major publisher of foundation directories, the Foundation Center's site extends your search. Contact: http://fdncenter.org. Not only do you find information about funding organizations, but you can view the free *Philanthropy News Digest* online to stay fully informed about the entire arena of philanthropy. See http://foundationcenter.org/pnd.

Foundation Directory. This is a great resource concerning 10,000 of the largest grant-making foundations in the United States. This edition includes seven indexes that include: (1) donors, officers and trustees; (2) geography; (3) international; (4) types of support; (5) subject; (6) new foundations; and (7) names. This is a useful index to pinpoint funders, especially at local or state levels.

Foundation Directory (**Part 2**). Part 2 describes foundations making annual awards between $50,000 and $199,000 each year and having assets of less than $2 million. Entries for 10,000 smaller foundations are included. Of interest to grant-seekers, over 85 percent of the donors specify some geographic limitation. This source is a good starter.

Foundation Grants Index. This summarizes over 100,000 grants of at least $10,000; thus grants awarded by foundations or corporations under that amount are excluded. This resource provides a comprehensive list of who got funded and by whom. By checking this source, you will know if you have a chance with over 1,000 different funders.

Foundation Grants to Individuals. One of the few guides that identify 8,300 entries for grants, scholarships, awards or honors for the individual. And you do not need an IRS 501 (c) (3) designation for most of the grants.

Foundations Online. Foundations Online is a service of the Northern California Community Foundation, Inc. However, its coverage is national in scope and has a specific website for charities. Again, this is a good starting point for identifying funding programs of non-profit groups: www.foundations.org/norcal.html.

Guide to Funding for International and Foreign Programs. This has a listing of over 2,000 potential funders for grant-seekers trying to locate foundation or corporate support for international programs. Statements of purpose, interests and types of funding are included with each entry.

National Directory of Corporate Giving: A Guide to Corporate Giving Programs and Corporate Funding. Profiled in this guide are 2,800 companies that regularly make contributions to non-profit groups. This directory is a must starting point when considering the solicitation of private sector funding. Further, the book has an extensive bibliographic listing of published papers about corporate funding.

Online Resources and Online Foundations. This is an ideal starting site to view a collection of online non-profit groups and funders plus many other resources. This website not only provides a listing of foundations, but also links to many federal documents, references and agencies. It even has a direct link to the Chronicle of Higher Education. www.findit.org/html/fund_online_foundations.html.

Online Funding Search Engines

COS PIVOT (previously Community of Science) is a subscription online search engine that brings together the principal investigator, the research administrator, the research development professionals, and internal and external experts outside of your institution. It has such features as: over 25,000 funding opportunities and alerts, pre-populated faculty profiles and assistance in identifying potential partnerships and collaborations. For more information, go to: www.refworks-cos.com/cospivot/Pivot_SinglePage_11x8.5_Online.pdf.

infoEd Global is a subscription online search engine that offers a variety of services for the principal investigators and researchers. SPIN and GENIUS are the two larger databases that provide funding opportunities and expertise management. SPIN is made up of over 40,000 funding programs (federal and non-federal) from 10,000 national and international agencies. GENIUS is a central database that provides the principal investigator's curriculum vitae and research profile, information updating, collaboration and reporting capabilities. Go to: http://infoedglobal.com for more information on services and costs.

In4Grants combines the quickness of a search engine, the familiarity of a social-media site and the power of application software. It provides a centralized workspace that makes grant discovery, peer collaboration and workflow tracking very easy. In4Grants services are explained in more detail at: www.in4grants.com.

SciVal Funding is a new funding search engine. One of its major features is to pull keywords from the researchers' publications. This site also offers expertise profiles, over 14,000 funding opportunities and 4,000 agency spotlights, plus a database listing more than $2.44 million in awards. There is a cost involved accessing this site. To find out more information, go to: www.scival.com.

ASSOCIATED ORGANIZATIONS

National Council of University Research Administrators (NCURA) is an organization of individuals with professional interests in the administration of sponsored programs (research, education and training), primarily at colleges and universities. NCURA's goals are to: (1) promote the development of more effective policies and procedures relative to the administration of sponsored programs to assure the achievement of the maximum potential in academic programs; (2) provide a forum through national and regional meetings for the discussion and exchange of information and experiences related to sponsored programs in colleges and universities; (3) disseminate current information and exchange of views on mutual concerns; and (4) provide professional development for college and university research administrators. info@ncura.edu.

Society of Research Administrators International (SRA) has an outstanding website. Perhaps this might be your very first entry for exploring possibilities to fund your ideas. SRA provides a virtual conspectus of federal and non-governmental sites, sources, products and services. If you need an OMB circular, you'll find it here. Several electronic publications are also listed. It is found at: info@srainternational.org.

COMPILING YOUR OWN LIST: BOOKMARKS

The number of websites maintained by other non-profit groups, businesses and corporations is staggering. As you surf for funds, add bookmarks for useful and interesting sites. Bookmarks will keep you anchored as you cast wide your web for grant support.

Bibliography

Bloom, B. S. (1984). "The 2 Sigma Problem: The Search for Methods of Group Instruction as Effective as One-to-One Tutoring," *Educational Researcher*, 13(6): 4–16.

Cohen, J. (1988). *Statistical Power Analysis for the Behavioral Sciences*, 2nd ed. Hillsdale, NH: Lawrence Erlbaum.

Cook, D. L. (1978). *Program Evaluation and Review Technique*. Lanham, MD: University Press of America.

Eisner, E. W. (March 1984). "Can Educational Research Inform Educational Practice?" *Phi Delta Kappan*, 65(7): 447–52.

Frechtling, J. W., et. al. (2002, January). *The 2002 User Friendly Handbook for Project Evaluation*. Washington, DC: National Science Foundation; Directorate for Education and Human Resources; Division of Research, Evaluation and Communications.

Glaser, R. (1963). "Instructional Technology and the Measurement of Learning Outcomes: Some Questions," *American Psychologist*, 18: 519–21.

Glass, G. V. (1976). "Primary, Secondary and Meta Analysis of Research," *Educational Researcher* 5(11): 3–8.

Glass, G. V. (1980). "Summarizing Effect Sizes," in R. Rosenthal (ed.), *New Directions for Methodology of Social and Behavioral Science: Quantitative Assessment of Research Domain*, San Francisco, CA: Jossey-Bass.

Gulick, L. H. and L. F. Urwick. (1937). *Papers on the Science of Administration*. New York: Columbia University Press.

Hattie, J. C. (2009). *Visible Learning: A Synthesis of Over 800 Meta-Analyses Relating to Achievement*. London and New York: Routledge/Taylor & Francis.

Helmer, O. (1967). *Analysis of the Future: The Delphi Method*. Santa Monica, CA: Rand Corporation.

House, E. R. (1978). "Assumptions Underlying Evaluation Models," *Educational Researcher*, 7(3): 4–12.

Kelly, T. F. (1991). *Practical Strategies for School Improvement*. Wheeling, IL: National School Services.

Lieberman, M. (1956). *Education as a Profession*. Englewood Cliffs, NJ: Prentice-Hall.

Marzano, R.J., D. J. Pickering and J. E. Pollack (2001). *Classroom Instruction That Works: Research-Based Strategies for Increasing Student Achievement*. Arlington, VA: ASCD.

Orlich, D. C. (1987). *Findings from In-Service Education Research for Elementary Science Teaching*. Washington, DC: Council for Elementary Science International, Monograph and Occasional Paper Series, No. 2, National Science Teachers Association.

Scriven, M. (1967). *The Methodology of Evaluation*. AERA Monograph Series on Curriculum Evaluation, No. 1: 39–83.

Stufflebeam, D. L. and A. J. Shinkfield (2007). *Evaluation Theory, Models and Application*. San Francisco, CA: Jossey-Bass.

Walberg, H. J. (1991). "Productive Teaching and Instruction: Assessing the Knowledge Base," in H. C. Waxman and H. J. Walberg (eds.), *Effective Teaching: Current Research*, Berkeley, CA: McCutchan Publishing, for the National Society for the Study of Education.

Additional References for Writing Effective Proposals

Bauer, D. G. (2008). *The "How To" Grants Manual: Successful Grantseeking Techniques for Obtaining Public and Private Grants*, 6th ed. Westport, CN: Praeger. Bauer is a premier grant proposal writer and has authored several other books and a series of ten videotapes on the topic.

Brewer, E. W. and C. M. Achilles (2008). *Funding Funding: Grant Writing from Start to Finish, Including Project Management and Internet Use*. Thousand Oaks, CA: Corwin Press. This book examines federal funding sources in detail, plus the many aspects of proposal writing. The authors show how to develop a competitive proposal.

Morrison, D. C. and S. V. Russell (N.D.) *The Grant Application Writer's Workbook: Successful Proposals to Any Agency*. P.O. Box 957, Los Olivos, CA 93441–0957. The authors focus on federal agencies; with copious notes.

Przeworski, A. and F. Solomon (2006). *The Art of Writing Proposals: Some Candid Suggestions for Applicants to Social Science Research Council Competitions*. Brooklyn: Social Science Research Council. On-line at: www.ucop.edu/acadadv/ppfp/documents/writing proposals.pdf. This provides a quick summary of what is needed for funding.

Reif-Lehrer, L. (2005). *Grant Application Writer's Handbook*. Sudbury, MA: Jones and Bartlett. This is a must for researchers who are seeking NIH funding. The author covers all details from idea generation to renewing an application.

Index